East-West Trade at a Crossroads:

Economic Relations with the Soviet Union and Eastern Europe

A Task Force Report
to the Trilateral Commission

Authors: Robert V. Roosa
Partner
Brown Brothers Harriman & Co.

Armin Gutowski
President
Hamburg Institute for Economic Research (HWWA)

Michiya Matsukawa
Senior Advisor to the President
Nikko Securities

Associate Author: William M. Reichert
Brown Brothers Harriman & Co.

Published by
NEW YORK UNIVERSITY PRESS
New York and London
1982

This report has been prepared for the Trilateral Commission. A first draft, completed March 12, 1982, was discussed at the Trilateral Commission meeting in Tokyo on April 4-6. Subsequently, a first revision, reflecting that discussion, was completed on May 28 for limited circulation. This final version was completed on July 9. The authors, who are from North America, Japan, and Western Europe, have been free to present their own views; and the opinions expressed are put forth in a personal capacity and do not purport to represent those of the Commission or of any organization with which the authors are associated.

© Copyright, 1982. The Trilateral Commission

Library of Congress Cataloging in Publication Data

Roosa, Robert V.
    East-West trade at a crossroads.

    (The Triangle papers ; 24)
    1. East-West trade (1945-   ) I. Gutowski, Armin. II. Matsukawa, Michiya, 1924-
        III. Trilateral Task Force on Economic Relations with the Soviet Union and Eastern
Europe. IV. Trilateral Commission. V. Title. VI. Series.
HF1411.R634   1982   382'.091713'01717   82-13364
ISBN 0-8147-7385-0
        0-8147-7386-9 (pbk.)

Manufactured in the United States of America

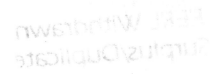

The Authors

ROBERT V. ROOSA is a partner of Brown Brothers Harriman & Co., which he joined in 1965 after service in the U.S. Government as UnderSecretary of the Treasury for Monetary Affairs (1961-64). Educated at the University of Michigan (Ph.D. in Economics), Mr. Roosa taught economics at Michigan, Harvard, and M.I.T., and served in the U.S. Army from 1943 to 1946 before joining the Federal Reserve Bank of New York in 1946, where he rose to Vice President of the Research Department in 1955-60. Mr. Roosa is a director of several corporations and other institutions. He has acted as Chairman of the Economics Panel of the long-standing U.S.-USSR Parallel Studies Program organized by the United Nations Associations of the United States and the Soviet Union. His many publications include *Money, Trade and Economic Growth* (editor, 1951), *Monetary Reform for the World Economy* (1965), and *The Dollar and World Liquidity* (1967).

MICHIYA MATSUKAWA had a long and distinguished career in the Japanese Ministry of Finance before assuming his current position in 1980 as Senior Advisor to the President of the Nikko Securities Company and Chairman of the Institute of the Nikko Research Center. Educated at Tokyo Imperial University (Faculty of Law, degree in political science) and the University of Illinois (M.A. in Economics), Mr. Matsukawa joined the Ministry of Finance in 1947. Rising through the ranks (including service in the New York consulate in 1960-61 and Washington embassy in 1965-68), he became Director-General of the International Finance Bureau in 1973-74, Deputy Vice Minister in 1974-75, Director-General of the Finance Bureau in 1975-76, and then Vice Minister for International Affairs in 1976-78. In 1978-80, he was Special Advisor to the Minister of Finance.

ARMIN GUTOWSKI is President of the HWWA — Institute for Economic Research — Hamburg, and Professor of Economics (international economic policy) at the University of Hamburg, positions he has held since 1978. In 1970-78, he was a member of the Council of Economic Experts of the Federal Republic and also Professor of Economics (money and international finance) at the University of Frankfurt. Educated at the Universities of Nuremberg, Hamburg, and Mainz, Dr. Gutowski was associated with the Research Institute of Political Economy at the University of Mainz in 1952-66, and with the University of Giessen in 1967-70. He was Chief Economic Advisor to the Kreditanstalt für Wiederaufbau in 1967-79. Dr. Gutowski's many publications include *Konglomerate, Unternehmungsgrösse und wirtschaftliche Macht* (1971), *International Monetary Problems* (co-author, 1972), and "Chances for Stability in Various International Monetary Systems" (1975).

*   *   *

WILLIAM M. REICHERT (Associate Author) began work with Robert V. Roosa at Brown Brothers Harriman & Co. in the summer of 1981, after receiving his M.B.A degree from the Stanford Graduate School of Business. Mr. Reichert received his B.A. degree, *magna cum laude*, from Harvard College in 1976. He worked for three years with McKinsey & Company in Los Angeles before enrolling at Stanford. He has also worked as a consultant to the World Bank, participating in a mission to Tanzania.

The Trilateral Process

The report which follows is the joint responsibility of the three authors, with Robert V. Roosa serving as principal drafter. Although only the authors are responsible for the analysis and conclusions, they have been aided in their work by many others. The persons consulted spoke for themselves as individuals and not as representatives of any organization with which they are associated.

On the North American side, of particular assistance have been *John P. Hardt*, Associate Director for Senior Specialists of the Congressional Research Service, and *Kate S. Tomlinson*, Senior Research Assistant at the Congressional Research Service. Hardt and Tomlinson prepared background papers in the autumn of 1981 on CoCom and on American sanctions after the Soviet invasion of Afghanistan, and made many helpful criticisms and comments on early drafts. *David Swanson* of Continental Grain and *James Giffen* of Armco Inc. were also particularly helpful. Consultations were carried out with a number of officials in the Departments of Agriculture, Commerce, and State. *Roger Hill*, Executive Secretary of the Canadian Group in the Trilateral Commission, provided a wealth of material related to Canada.

On the Japanese side, several meetings were held with persons from various Japanese companies, trading companies in particular; and consultations were held with officials of the Ministries of Foreign Affairs, Finance, and International Trade and Industry. Particular assistance has been provided by *Eisuke Sakakibara*, Director of the Research Division of the International Finance Bureau at the Japanese Ministry of Finance; *Yasushi Sakurai*, Director of the Economic Cooperation Department at the Keidanren; *Kazuo Ogawa*, Director, Department of Economic Studies, Japan Association for Trade with the U.S.S.R. and Eastern European Countries; and *Takao Sebata*, Program Officer, Research and Documentation, Japan Center for International Exchange.

On the European side, particular assistance has been provided by three members of the staff of the Hamburg Institute for Economic Research (HWWA): *Klaus Bolz*, Head of the Department for Socialist Countries and East-West Economic Relations; *Petra Pissula*, in charge of Eastern European countries in the same department; and *Dieter-Georg Lösch* of the Special Projects Department attached to the Office of the President. Others consulted included *Giovanni Agnelli*, President of

FIAT; *Diether Hoffmann*, then Speaker of the Executive Board of the Bank für Gemeinwirtschaft; *Michael Kaser*, Professor of Economics, Oxford University; *John Maslen*, Relations with State-Trading Countries, Directorate-General for External Relations, Commission of the European Communities; *Richard Portes*, Birbeck College of the University of London; *Giuseppe Ratti*, Coordinator, International Affairs, ENI, Rome; *José Antonio Segurado*, Vice Chairman, CEOE (Spanish Confederation of Enterprises) and Chairman of SEFISA in Madrid; *Lord Shackleton*, Deputy Chairman, Rio-Tinto Zinc Corporation Ltd., and former Cabinet Minister; *Georges Sokoloff*, CEPII (Centre d'Etude Prospectives et Informations Internationales), French Commissariat du Plan; *Janez Stanovnik*, Executive Secretary, United Nations Economic Commission for Europe; *Otto Wolff von Amerongen*, President, Otto Wolff AG, and President, German Federation of Chambers of Industry and Commerce; and *Stephen Woolcock*, Royal Institute of International Affairs. *Paul Révay*, the European Secretary of the Trilateral Commission, was also of great assistance.

Consultations were carried out with Soviet experts by Robert Roosa in June 1981 in Moscow and in January 1982 in the United States. Several consultations with Eastern European experts were also held by each of the authors.

All three authors express their appreciation for the extraordinary help of *William M. Reichert* of Brown Brothers Harriman & Co., who not only provided research support, but also drafted some sections and provided editorial assistance throughout. *Elizabeth Campbell's* assistance was invaluable as copy editor, coordinator, and typist. *Barbara Keller* worked indefatigably with Ms. Campbell and the authors on all aspects of processing the material. *Gene Insogna* was of great help in preparing the text exhibits. The New York staff of the Trilateral Commission — *George Franklin, Charles Heck,* and *Daniel Newman* — has been extremely helpful throughout this study in all aspects, ranging from editorial comments to logistical arrangements. Mr. Heck has also made important substantive contributions to the completed text.

Table of Contents

Exhibits

INTRODUCTION:
PERSPECTIVE ON EAST-WEST RELATIONS

The alternating waves of amity and antagonism between East and West since World War II have not yet produced among the Trilateral countries[1] a comprehensive strategic policy for future relations with the Soviet Union and Eastern Europe. Perhaps the approach must continue to be only a wary eclecticism. Whatever may be in the making, it seems clear that economic factors and forces have not thus far been woven consistently or effectively into the strands of political and military policy with which the Western allies seems to be wrestling.

Too often in the past, any forward planning of grand strategy that has been attempted has been in terms of military objectives, control over nuclear or conventional armaments, and political relations between the Trilateral and CMEA[2] countries, individually or collectively. Strategy, in the sense of any longer term, carefully developed Western consensus, has tended to neglect or to override economic dimensions. Yet actual developments have at times caused Western countries to resort to forms of economic pressure against the East. The consequence has been precipitate action, with little coordination, applied in ways that proved relatively ineffective or counterproductive. Governments have also frequently discovered too late that the scope for political maneuver in the implementation of policy has been seriously limited by economic constraints.

Without suggesting what all of the other strands of overall strategy should be, this study attempts to outline an approach in trade and financial affairs which might be suitable for any Western strategic

---

[1] The Trilateral countries are the industrialized countries of Western Europe and North America, as well as Japan. For convenience in this study, and disregarding geographical location, they are often referred to as "the West." For statistical purposes, the Trilateral countries are often equated with the Organization for Economic Cooperation and Development (OECD), unless otherwise specified.
[2] The "East" is often used as a convenient abbreviation for seven members of the Council for Mutual Economic Assistance (CMEA): the Soviet Union and the six countries referred to throughout as "Eastern Europe," i.e., Bulgaria, Czechoslovakia, the German Democratic Republic (GDR), Hungary, Poland, and Romania. Cuba, Mongolia, and Vietnam are not included in the CMEA for the purposes of this study.

doctrine on relations with the East that presumes: 1) an overriding need to maintain peaceful conditions, 2) a continuing need for a balanced stand-off in military capability, and 3) an unrelenting rivalry between the two sides in attempting to extend the influence of their competing political systems.

By 1982 it has become a recognized truism that "detente," whatever it may have meant in earlier years to the statesmen or the populations of either side, has lost its original lustre in the West. One of the more romantic popular visions of detente had been the belief, or the hope, that the Soviet Union — following the series of agreements during the 'sixties and 'seventies on nuclear testing, arms control, space exploration, and scientific and cultural exchange, as well as the development of closer economic ties — would no longer cross the threshold of military aggression in seeking to strengthen its external bases of political and strategic power. Disillusionments kept recurring even during these years, but a compelling "last straw" for many came with the entry of Soviet troops into Afghanistan at the end of 1979. Another divisive development was the imposition of martial law in Poland on December 13, 1981.

The question for the future is whether there can at some time be a revival of detente in a more viable form, based on a realistic understanding of the differences between the two political systems. The expectation must be that active rivalry will continue, but hopefully within a framework of normal diplomatic exchange and stable military equilibrium. That kind of detente would not impair existing political or military or economic alliances, nor weaken any nation's safeguards on its own unique technology, but it would encourage the expansion of those ordinary commercial and financial relations from which each side could expect an advantage, and from which neither need suffer a disadvantage. Such a relationship would not preclude, in extreme circumstances, the curtailment of some economic relations for a time in response to a serious threat or violation of trust, but it would not include a deliberate curtailment of economic intercourse in the mistaken belief that the adversary could be permanently weakened. Moreover, a new detente would recognize the potential for mutual gains in a widening of the scope for market determination of prices in trade between East and West.

This study examines the possibilities for constructive economic relations between the Trilateral West and the CMEA East in the current environment. At the risk of omitting Hamlet from the play, there has been no attempt to deal with broader political and strategic issues, most notably the scale and nature of the arms race between the USSR

2

and the U.S., or between the Warsaw Pact and NATO. Quite obviously, though, the intricate complexities of any arms limitation agreements that may be reached, or the failure to reach an accord, must have a most profound impact on the economic performance of both sides. The full range of that potential impact cannot be encompassed in a survey focused primarily on trade and finance.

Indeed the year 1982, in which this study is being completed, presents a paradoxical picture of confusion in both political and economic relations. Lengthy exchanges still take place between the diplomats and negotiators in Madrid and Geneva, at the United Nations, and through the media, though often in a combative tone; economic sanctions against the Soviet Union are being applied doggedly though erratically by the United States and some other Western countries; but meanwhile the United States is an eager seller of grain to the East, and leading countries of Western Europe contract for new supplies of Soviet natural gas in return for supplying large credits to finance pipeline facilities produced in the West. Underneath all of this, on both sides, there are suspicions of motives and fears of an accidental stumbling into nuclear war. This is not, it would seem, a propitious time to be surveying the scope for fruitful expansion of trade and financial relations.

Yet the authors of this study do find some prospects for an orderly passage through the confusion. The starting point is to recognize forthrightly that the potential for economic contacts between Trilateral and CMEA countries cannot be explored in the same terms that apply among the countries of the West. Aside from the fundamental problems of political and military competition, there is also a continuing problem of translation between economic systems that cope in quite different ways with the cost-benefit issues that arise in the allocation of resources among alternative uses. That is, methods of valuation, and the criteria for determining actual comparative advantage, must be different for a system where business decisions are determined by the mandate of a central plan from those for a system where decisions on prices and costs are reached through the guidance of market forces. Nonetheless, partly because the sluggish economies in both the East and the West currently call for new initiatives in trade, and also because longer term prospects during the decade of the 'eighties and beyond point to a compatibility between the resources and needs of the East and the West, there are compelling reasons — even with full recognition of the necessary constraints — for trying to enlarge the spread of the international division of labor among the Trilateral and CMEA countries.

3

There were substantial gains of this nature during the 'seventies, the decade of detente. Aggregate East-West trade (exports plus imports) rose nearly six-fold in nominal terms from 1970 through 1979, although with wide variations among countries and years.[1] The overall proportions of this trade in comparison to the estimated GNPs of both sides, while still small, also rose. Although there was some slackening in the pace of the real growth of GNP on both sides later in the decade, the enlarged trade may have helped to keep the decline from going further, particularly for a few countries in Western Europe.

It is with some of this history that the study begins. Section I describes the trends of trade and capital flows between the Trilateral countries and the CMEA countries during the postwar period. It focuses particularly on the more specific dimensions and characteristics of that trade since 1970. How has it been financed? What have been the growth and investment patterns in the CMEA? And what are some of the implications of the most recent developments — Afghanistan and Poland — for the policies and actions of the Trilateral countries?

After this broad survey, there will be a more detailed view in Section II of the key economic sectors in which future expansion, if any, might be expected to occur. What are the costs and benefits for the East and the West of continuing, to the extent economically profitable, along the lines of mutual trade expansion that evolved during the '70s? Might a growing interdependence put the West in an exposed position, vulnerable to economic pressures from the East, or might it perhaps create new strains among the Trilateral countries? Do the purely operational difficulties of doing business with the centrally planned economies place serious limits on future expansion? What are the implications of the current overindebtedness of Poland and Romania? Is it possible that mutually profitable commercial exchanges might in the longer run, despite the disappointment thus far, lead to greater political understanding and trust? In any case, what are the comparative advantages, for either the West or the East, in such economic sectors as

---

[1] Data used throughout this study are taken from what are believed to be reliable sources. However, specific data have often been difficult to reconcile owing to differences among the sources in definitions and in reference dates. Where complex reconciliations were required to present data in a reasonably homogeneous form, no attempt has been made to attach footnotes indicating the detailed variety of sources or data adjustments. The aim of the study is not to provide new formulations of statistical material but instead to utilize available data to aid a general analysis of major developments and prospects. The record of what happened to trade, and of actions to promote or obstruct trade, during the postwar period up through the 'seventies, particularly with respect to the USSR and the U.S., is not only documented in many Western studies, to some of which reference is made later, but also in E. S. Shershnev, *On the Principle of Mutual Advantage* (Moscow: Progress Publishers, 1978).

energy, agriculture, technology and manufactures, services (e.g., shipping and insurance), and finance (both for trade and investment)?

Following that rather clinical diagnosis, the third and final focus will be on practical policies for the future. What kinds of restraints or boundaries should the West put on a general expansion of economic relationships — either to control strategically critical exports, or to impose temporary sanctions in support of foreign policy objectives? Conversely, with controls in place over sensitive relations, what governmental initiatives would be appropriate for actually encouraging useful trade outside the restricted zone? Or might encouragement go too far, leading the East to a position of economic parity that could lessen economic pressures on the USSR to agree to limit or reduce armaments? What scope might there be, in any furthering or conditioning of Trilateral relations with the economies of the CMEA countries, for such international institutions as the International Monetary Fund (IMF), the General Agreement on Tariffs and Trade (GATT), the Organization for Economic Cooperation and Development (OECD), and the Bank for International Settlements (BIS)? What are the potentials for private initiative, within the context of conducting business with an often complex and procrastinating bureaucracy? Do prospects differ significantly among the CMEA countries? More broadly, how can the Trilateral countries, within the context of their relations with the CMEA countries, most effectively promote their own growth while also preserving Western values and democratic institutions?

Initially, it is important to outline several basic propositions which have emerged during the course of this study:

- The West cannot quarantine the East economically; economic relations at some level are certain to continue.
- The West cannot, through any practicable effort to coordinate its economic leverage, prevent the East's economic growth, although it may possibly slow the pace of some elements of that growth.
- The West may be able to delay for a time particular weapons developments in the East by denying access to certain technologies, but it cannot prevent the East from eventually acquiring or equaling whatever technology is available in the West.
- The West must recognize that the extension of economic relations with the East will not lead any of the CMEA countries into a political alignment with the West.
- The West can confidently expect to remain economically stronger than the East, regardless of how much trade expands, because of the inherently superior capacity for innovation and development

5

resulting from the comparatively free rein given to individual initiative in the West's economic system.

- The West should be able to expand two-way non-military trade with the East during periods of stable political relations, subject to the desirability common to all countries of so diversifying trade as to avoid undue dependence upon any one source or outlet.
- The West should be prepared, when political conditions permit, to extend credit on non-concessional terms in support of trade with individual Eastern countries, as their debt servicing capacity and performance may justify.
- The West can hope that mutually beneficial trade relations, as and if they develop, will help provide an atmosphere conducive to constructive negotiations aimed at
  — reaching enforceable agreements that assure a stable military equilibrium between East and West, and
  — reducing the military burdens that now divert so large a proportion of the economic resources of most countries on both sides away from productive uses and the meeting of human needs.

Briefly to foreshadow the study as a whole, a major underlying theme is that the sheer facts of economic geography and human resources in the Trilateral and the CMEA countries, were it not for their basic political differences, would impel a broad two-way flow of materials, products, and services between these vast areas. Political and strategic considerations inescapably limit the extent to which these economic potentials can be realized. That is why, after reviewing the remarkable trade expansion that did occur under the umbrella of detente during the 'seventies (Section I), and after considering some of the potentials that might lie ahead along many of the same lines (Section II), this study has focused in Section III on the kinds of boundaries on trade that need to be drawn by the West.

The analysis does suggest that the West can, without weakening its own relative strength, realize some economic gains from a renewed expansion of trading relations with the East during the course of this decade. The key premise is that any increase in trade, if it is to occur, must be mutually beneficial. There may be a further useful carryover if greater trade improves the climate for political relations.

Yet it should be equally clear that the West must place effective limits on any development in economic relations that could seriously weaken its own strategic position, or uniquely advance the strategic or military capability of the East. That is why the study takes a close look at the existing arrangements among the NATO countries and Japan for control over trade with the East in highly sophisticated technology or weapons (that is, through the CoCom, the Committee for the Control of the Export of Strategic Commodities). Such controls, preferably through a system of treaties, should be strengthened, sharpened, and adapted to the current need for control over the transfer of unique scientific processes as well as products.

Given such a specific and effective check on transfers of critical technology, the way should then be open for a renewed development of trade, with the approval of Western governments, subject to three other policy constraints on which the Trilateral governments should negotiate understandings: 1) the possible but rare, selective, and coordinated use of sanctions or embargoes on the sale of particular goods or on the extension of credits, for the purpose of penalizing or deterring specific aggression; 2) the prudent need to maintain a diversification among sources and markets as trade with the East grows; and 3) restraint on the use of concessional terms in trade or finance.

As for sanctions, this study finds that their use thus far has been of limited effectiveness. They may have helped to amplify diplomatic protests against the aggressive actions of others, but their punitive impact on aggressors has been slight and their disruptive impact on the sanction-imposing countries substantial. A better approach, so far as the possible use of sanctions by the West against the East is concerned, would be to work toward an understanding among the Trilateral countries — perhaps within the CoCom framework — on the conditions for imposing sanctions in the future, including some sharing of the costly burdens of such sanctions among those countries. The mere existence of such an understanding may help as a deterrent to future aggression and should provide powerful support for diplomatic initiatives, perhaps thereby avoiding an actual invoking of sanctions, and at the least assuring meaningful consultation among allies before any precipitate use of sanctions.

Some who are critical of the approach taken in this study would instead go much further in politically constraining or shaping Trilateral-CMEA economic relations. At the extreme, there are some, particularly in the United States, who would want to virtually shut down economic relations with the Soviet Union in a kind of undeclared economic warfare. As will already be quite obvious, this is emphatically not the authors' view. Soviet autarky is sufficiently powerful to thwart any attempt to force a collapse of the Soviet system through economic action. If instead there were an effort to use trade mainly as a tool for leverage to weaken or manipulate the other CMEA countries, there would be a grave risk of creating a new fortress mentality among

7

the CMEA countries with unpredictable consequences in the decades ahead.

The approach of this study is instead to set certain constraints or boundaries — of the varieties mentioned above — with economic relations then relatively free to run their course outside of those limits. That seems to the authors to be the best and most practicable way to give political guidance to East-West economic relations.

For other critics, this is still not enough. They would want Western governments to look more deeply into the political impact in the Soviet Union of economic relations "outside the boundaries" and actively use these economic relations to shape Soviet development and overall relations. They speak aggressively of a political "strategy" for the use of economic relations to leverage down the rate of economic growth in the East, in contrast to this study's more modest approach, which limits any deliberate restriction of the non-sensitive trade to the use of sanctions only in very unusual circumstances.

The lines of argument of these critics often begin by citing the decline in the rate of growth of the Soviet economy; some observers describe this as a growing crisis of the Soviet economic system. Some critics in the West relate the decline in growth in large part to investment in military strength, so that the capital investment which would be required for growth is crowded out. Is it a wise Western strategy, they ask, to help fill this investment gap, and thus to make it easier for the Soviet Union to overcome its declining growth rate? Others would put more stress on a technology gap rather than an investment gap, but ask a similar question concerning the transfer of technology through trade. Some take this argument one step further and contend that Western economic ties, by reducing internal pressures to shift resources to civilian economic growth, would help the Soviet Union to devote larger amounts of its resources to military power.

The authors' sense of Soviet decision-making, however, is that military "requirements" will always be met ahead of civilian consumption, and that any gain in Soviet production related to East-West trade will largely accrue to the general public. Moreover, it is important not to overestimate the unique contribution of economic relations with the West to the Soviet growth rate. On balance, the gain, though modest, should be as great for the West as for the East. Beyond that qualification is another significant consideration. The implementing of any strategy for treating the USSR and Eastern Europe as pariahs by putting a blight on general trade — quite apart from the problem of getting intra-Trilateral agreement on undertaking such an approach — would break down over the problems both of defining the kinds of goods or credits to constrict, and of maintaining a coordinated and sustained compliance.

The alternative of using the crude tactics of across-the-board embargoes on the major categories of trade, moreover, would stand little chance of wide Trilateral support, would be circumvented by countries outside the Trilateral circle, and would risk degeneration into the sort of outright economic warfare that the advocates of influence through economic strategy would presumably wish to avoid. All in all, the authors are persuaded that the suggestions in this study for concentrating on various limited constraints or boundaries represent the most practicable way to define the political guidelines for trade.

Another kind of argument made with regard to Western political control of economic relations "outside the boundaries" is that Western governments should be more actively involved in these transactions, suggesting for example that loans should be made only with government guarantees and government permission. The authors recognize and support the need for thorough government monitoring of economic relations with the Soviet Union and Eastern Europe, but to require governmental permission and guarantees for all or most credits and exports "outside the boundaries" would be a shift toward the techniques of the command economy. The Trilateral countries might paradoxically risk, in that way, a drift into use of the very methods which their policies are presumably designed to oppose.

The authors' conclusion is that, outside the necessary constraints, there can be useful economic gains for the West, and that these gains can reinforce political objectives. It is, to be sure, naïve to believe that trade expansion necessarily brings peace, or that economic inducements alone could lead the Soviet Union to give up any efforts to extend its external bases of political and strategic power. Nor should the West expect, as mentioned earlier, that the extension of economic relations will lead any of the East European countries into a political alignment with the West.

The general aim should be to develop along any non-sensitive lines that are clearly supportive of economic growth and expansion in the West, so long as practicable alternatives would be available if serious interruptions were to occur in East-West relations. Running through all of the analysis of this study, moreover, is recognition of the great comparative advantage that the West enjoys because of its reliance upon the dynamism of its free and flexible market economies. That is the West's greatest assurance of continued strength, regardless of how much or how little occurs in the future expansion of trade and credit flows with the East.

9

The succeeding sections of this study outline the results of the authors' efforts, with the help of many others whose contributions are acknowledged in a prefatory note, to identify the kinds of constructive East-West economic relations that may develop whenever the tensions and strains of early 1982 subside. The study will follow the outline already indicated: (I) East-West Economic Relations since World War II; (II) Potentials and Problems in Key Economic Sectors; and (III) The Realistic Prospects for Trilateral Policy.

I. East-West Economic Relations Since World War II

A. TRENDS IN TRADE

The large wartime deliveries to the Soviet Union and Eastern Europe from the United States began to taper off with the decline of UNRRA (United Nations Relief and Rehabilitation Administration) assistance in 1945. The first of the postwar cycles of ascending and descending economic relations began in October of that year when a special U.S. credit agreement was made to support the re-tooling of the Soviet economy; it was suspended at the end of 1946. The deterioration of East-West relations in 1946, and the onset of the Cold War after 1947 — following the Soviet Union's brusque rejection of proposals to extend the Marshall Plan to areas in its sphere of influence — brought economic relations between East and West to a bare minimum, despite the signing of a bilateral trade and financial agreement between the United Kingdom and the USSR at the close of 1947.

Meanwhile the Soviet Union, conditioned both by its Marxist-Leninist philosophy and by its centuries-old fear of hostile encirclement, was consolidating its dominance over the six countries of Eastern Europe, forming them into a virtual frontier barrier against the West during the earlier postwar years. The CMEA was formally established in January 1949, while the USSR and East Germany were enforcing the Berlin blockade from mid-1948 to mid-1949. The resulting tensions in the West led to the North Atlantic Alliance in April 1949 and the founding of the North Atlantic Treaty Organization (NATO) in 1951. A policy of trade embargo by the United States, West Germany, and others at the close of the '40s was countered by a Soviet policy of autarky for itself and the countries of Eastern Europe, emphasizing self-sufficiency and integration within the Soviet system. Consequently, Western trade with the Soviet Union and other Eastern countries was reduced to nominal amounts through most of the 1950s. Toward the end of that decade, there was a gradual but small rise in trade by some Western European countries. Following Stalin's death in 1953, and particularly during the Khrushchev era from 1957 to 1964, Canada and Japan also increased their trade with the East intermittently.

Nonetheless, by 1961 the total trade turnover of all OECD countries[1] with the seven CMEA countries equaled only $4.3 billion, representing barely 2.4 percent of the total world trade of the OECD countries. (See Exhibit 1 for greater detail on the development of East-West trade.) On the other hand, trade with the West represented about 21 percent of the total trade of CMEA countries during the early 1960s; but trade was a much smaller factor in their economies because autarky had made for slower progress among the Eastern countries in the development of diversification, and of specialization along lines of comparative economic advantage, in contrast with the West. The consequence was a growing frustration in the East, as the CMEA countries became increasingly aware of the more rapid advances in the West that followed from the momentum generated initially by the Marshall Plan and later by the expansion of free trade within Western Europe.

In 1964 the CMEA countries, under Soviet leadership, attempted to multilateralize trade among themselves more effectively by creating a clearing bank, the International Bank for Economic Cooperation (IBEC). Nonetheless, during the later 'sixties there was a widening recognition among the CMEA countries that their centrally planned systems could not readily expand into higher levels of economic development without extending trade beyond the "socialist community" to gain access to new technologies and additional capital. Consequently, the older forms of autarky began to disappear. A new approach in 1971 took the form of a "Comprehensive Program" for the integration and development of the socialist economies. A start was made toward expanding the partial convertibility of the ruble among the CMEA countries through their accounts at the IBEC. And the International Investment Bank (IIB) was established in that same year by the CMEA to facilitate the long-term financing of joint development projects among its member countries. Together, the older and newer institutions aimed to coordinate economic planning among the seven countries, to create a stable trading currency, and to improve the flexibility of trade and capital flows among the CMEA countries. But the results of even that effort were soon disappointing. The outcome was that economic contact with the West became even more attractive,

---

[1]The OECD is a convenient proxy for those countries which are also described as the "Industrialized World" in UN statistics. Differences between these groups of Western countries are usually minor, but all statistical references are labeled accordingly.

and the usefulness of the IBEC and IIB came largely through their serving as a conduit for access to the hard currencies of the West.[1]

Meanwhile, during the '60s, the ability and the willingness of the United States to continue its restraints on CMEA trade weakened in the face of increasing opposition from Western Europe. From a very low base level of $4.3 billion in 1961, combined East-West exports and imports grew to $13.7 billion in 1970.[2] The growth of trade consisted mainly of imports of manufactures and capital goods by the CMEA, and of imports of fuels, agricultural products, raw materials, and some manufactures by the OECD. Still, trade was limited by intermittent tensions in East-West political relations during the '60s, and by 1971 total East-West trade was less than 3 percent of the total trade of the OECD countries, although it had risen to 25 percent of CMEA trade.

In the early '70s, political and economic factors combined to stimulate interest in exploring and developing new markets, including the expansion of East-West trade. One impelling economic factor in the West initially was economic recession which was reflected in a slowdown of trade. The overall export volume of the industrial countries grew less than half as fast in 1971 as it had in 1968.[3] Growth in the Soviet Union, too, began to slow down; the real growth rate in 1972 was the lowest in a decade.

The prime movers in the broadening of relations were, however, political forces. In Western Europe, North America, and Japan, growing concern over the proliferation of nuclear weapons was a major force strongly favoring a rapprochement — not only among the countries of Western Europe and those of the CMEA, but principally between the United States and the Soviet Union. The Limited Test Ban Treaty of 1963 was one early manifestation. As a result, such political and strategic considerations, along with awareness of economic potentialities, combined to give birth to detente.

President De Gaulle made a promising exploratory visit to the Soviet Union in 1966. The christening of detente may then have occurred with the beginning of West Germany's *Ostpolitik* toward the end of the 'sixties, followed by its treaties with Poland and the USSR. President Nixon's visit to Moscow in May 1972 (following a trip to Beijing) culminated extensive negotiations which were highlighted by the

---

[1]Lawrence J. Brainard, "CMEA Financial System and Integration,"*East European Integration and East-West Trade*, Paul Marer and J.M. Montias, eds. (Bloomington: Indiana University Press, 1980), pp.121-145.

[2]Unless otherwise noted, data are presented in current dollars.

[3]International Monetary Fund, *Annual Report 1973*, p. 18. The growth of industrial country exports was 5.9 percent in 1971 vs. 14.2 percent in 1968.

Exhibit 1

GROWTH OF EAST-WEST TRADE
1961-1979

CMEA Imports from OECD

Commodity Group	Value (million U.S. dollars)						Growth*		Pct. of Total		
	1961	1971	1973	1975	1977	1979	'61-71	'71-79	'61	'71	'79
Food and Beverages	311	860	2,613	3,458	3,318	6,880	10.7%	29.7%	15%	12%	18%
Crude Materials	217	499	1,146	1,240	1,699	2,904	8.7	24.6	10	7	8
Mineral Fuels	3	71	115	201	228	463	37.2	26.4	<1	1	1
Chemicals	191	832	1,347	2,839	3,395	4,805	15.9	24.5	9	12	13
Manufactured Goods	729	2,342	4,289	8,731	8,728	12,150	12.4	22.8	34	34	32
Machinery and Transportation Equip.	689	2,300	4,415	9,351	10,283	11,156	12.8	21.8	32	33	29
TOTAL	2,140	6,904	13,924	25,819	27,651	38,357	12.4	23.9	100	100	100

* compound annual growth rate

CMEA Exports to OECD

Commodity Group	Value (million U.S. dollars)						Growth*		Pct. of Total		
	1961	1971	1973	1975	1977	1979	'61-71	'71-79	'61	'71	'79
Food and Beverages	633	1,208	1,907	2,093	1,990	2,594	6.7%	10.0%	29%	18%	7%
Crude Materials	537	1,290	2,217	2,746	3,310	3,841	9.2	14.6	24	19	11
Mineral Fuels	412	1,533	2,337	6,455	8,745	15,300	14.0	33.3	19	23	44
Chemicals	125	357	552	927	1,523	2,487	11.1	27.5	6	5	7
Manufactured Goods	375	1,773	3,417	3,891	5.603	7,718	16.8	20.2	17	26	22
Machinery and Transportation Equip.	120	588	1,060	1,516	1,927	2,813	17.2	21.6	5	9	8
TOTAL	2,204	6,749	11,490	17,627	23,090	34,754	11.8	22.7	100	100	100

* compound annual growth rate

Note: Some columns do not add due to rounding and minor data collection errors.

Sources: OECD. *Statistics of Foreign Trade, Series C* (Paris: OECD, 1979); Eugene Zaleski and Helgard Wienert, *Technology Transfer between East and West*, (Paris: OECD, 1980) Table A-4, p. 313, Table A-5, pp. 314-15.

accords that were signed on subjects ranging from arms limitation (SALT I) to technical exchanges. The way was prepared during the President's visit for the broad U.S.-USSR trade agreement which was reached later in 1972. Meanwhile, Japan's trade relations with the USSR began shifting, triggered by three significant projects in Siberia concerned with forest resources, harbor construction, and pulp-making facilities. As a result, after years of relatively little trade and continuous deficits, Japan moved into surplus with the Soviet Union in 1975.

The era of detente brought about a rapid acceleration in the growth of East-West trade. From the CMEA countries, exports of fuels and chemicals grew at an especially fast pace (Exhibit 1); their imports from the OECD countries consisted mainly of capital goods, agricultural products, chemicals, and manufactures. Overall, total trade turnover between the CMEA and OECD countries rose from $13.7 billion in 1971 to $73.1 billion in 1979.[1] For the Western countries this represented 3.3 percent of total trade; for the CMEA, it was 30.3 percent of total trade (but in turn, trade for the CMEA countries on average was only half as important in relation to GNP as it was in the West). Even after allowing for the increasing pace of inflation over these years, the real volume of two-way trade approximately tripled over the decade.

B. THE CURRENT STRUCTURE OF TRADE

Trade between the East and the West did not expand homogeneously. For the West Europeans the major source of export growth during the 'seventies, both to the USSR and to Eastern Europe, was in machinery and transport equipment, manufactured goods in the form of iron and steel products, and chemicals. Western Europe's exports to Eastern Europe alone rose from $3.3 billion in 1970 to $15.7 billion in 1979, while exports to the Soviet Union rose from $2.0 billion to $11.7 billion during the same period. The United States and Canada sent most of their exports to the Soviet Union, and agricultural products overwhelmingly dominated these exports. Similarly, Japan sent an even higher proportion of its exports to the Soviet Union over the years 1974 through 1979 (Exhibit 2). It had not then and has not yet made a significant entry into the markets of Eastern Europe, in contrast with the success of its exports elsewhere in the world. The composition of Japan's exports, however, was strikingly similar to Western Europe's as typified by West Germany. (Exhibit 3 provides a breakdown highlighting the differences in 1979 in the volume and composition of exports to the CMEA

---

[1] In 1980, East-West trade turnover grew to $85.3 billion, dropping to $79.9 billion in 1981.

16

Exhibit 2

CMEA TRADE AS PERCENT OF
TOTAL TRADE OF TRILATERIAL COUNTRIES
(1974-1979 averages)

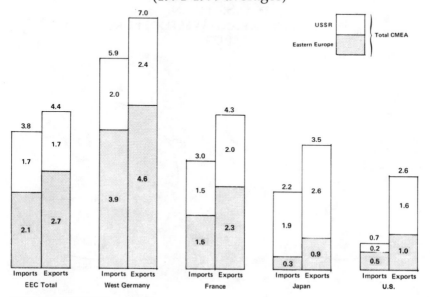

Source: U.S. Department of Commerce compilation of U.N. data.

countries by the United States, Japan, West Germany, and Western Europe as a whole, before U.S. sanctions following the Soviet move into Afghanistan distorted trade patterns.)

Imports from the CMEA countries show even more divergence among the Western countries (Exhibit 4). West Germany has been, as in the case of exports, the CMEA's largest single trading partner in the West. Excluding intra-German trade, combined trade between the CMEA countries and the Federal Republic totaled $16.7 billion in 1979, i.e., 5.1 percent of total West German trade. From the USSR alone, 69 percent of West German imports in 1979 consisted of fuels, but imports of chemicals (particularly radioactive materials), raw materials, and non-ferrous metals (for example, silver and nickel) have also been substantial. France and Italy also imported sizable quantities of fuels from the USSR (which provided 56 percent of Italy's gas imports in 1979), as well as such raw materials as pulpwood, timber, and cotton.

Western Europe's imports from Eastern Europe, excluding the USSR, showed a somewhat wider variety during the '70s: fuels, timber,

17

Exhibit 3

COMPOSITION OF EXPORTS TO CMEA
BY U.S., JAPAN,
WEST GERMANY AND WESTERN EUROPE
1979

U.S.

Total — $5.66 billion

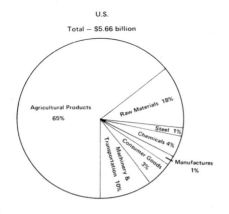

JAPAN

Total — $3.26 billion

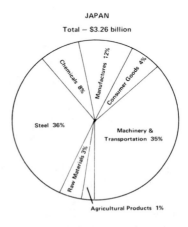

WESTERN EUROPE [a]

Total — $27.50 billion

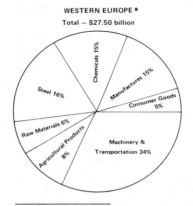

WEST GERMANY [a]

Total — $8.69 billion

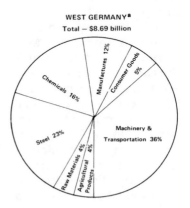

[a]Does not include intra-German trade
Note: Percentages may not total 100% due to rounding
Source: OECD, *Statistics of Foreign Trade, Series B* (Paris: OECD, 1979)

Exhibit 4

COMPOSITION OF IMPORTS FROM CMEA
BY U.S., JAPAN,
WEST GERMANY AND WESTERN EUROPE
1979

U.S.
Total — $1.43 billion

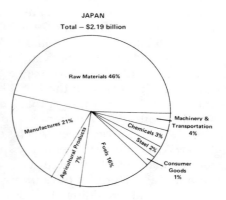

JAPAN
Total — $2.19 billion

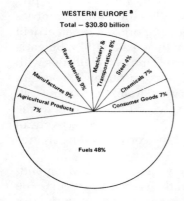

WESTERN EUROPE [a]
Total — $30.80 billion

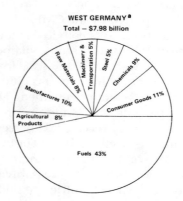

WEST GERMANY [a]
Total — $7.98 billion

[a]Does not include intra-German trade
Note: Percentages may not total 100% due to rounding
Source: OECD, *Statistics of Foreign Trade, Series B* (Paris: OECD, 1979)

simple iron and steel products, non-ferrous metals, textiles, special machinery and parts, and food. Japan, whose imports from the CMEA countries (including the USSR) totaled $2.19 billion in 1979 (about one-fourth of West Germany's imports), has been receiving mainly raw materials, such as timber and ores, which comprised 46 percent of its 1979 total. The United States has consistently been an even smaller importer, scattering its imports among a variety of categories.

The West European countries are by far the most important Western trading partners of the CMEA countries. The total of Western Europe's imports from the six Eastern European countries rose from $3.2 billion in 1970 to $14.5 billion in 1979, while its imports from the USSR rose from $2.0 billion to $16.3 billion. While there are several important categories of both exports to and imports from the USSR and Eastern Europe, careful examination suggests that, with the possible exception of energy imports from the USSR by some Western European countries, there is as yet no approach toward dependence by any of the Western countries on either the export markets or the products of the East. Even in the case of energy (as discussed further below in Section II, Part A), whatever vulnerability appears superficially to exist is in fact readily manageable through backstop arrangements — meanwhile permitting Western European countries to conserve their own energy reserves, and providing the East with some of the hard currency earnings essential for two-way trade.

On the other hand, the East is to a certain extent dependent on some imported Western products, notably special machinery, high quality iron and steel products, and replacement parts for machinery previously imported by the CMEA countries. All of the CMEA countries need export markets both to pay for needed imports and to meet debt service on the sizable credits obtained from the West. In 1979, Bulgaria was at the lower end of the scale for Eastern European countries with only 14 percent of her exports going to OECD countries and 15 percent of her imports coming from them. Hungary and Romania, by contrast, sent 34 percent and 33 percent, respectively, of their exports to the West, while they received 38 percent and 39 percent, respectively, of their imports from the West. For the USSR the corresponding figures were 30 percent and 35 percent in 1979.

These figures do not necessarily imply, however, a critical dependence of the CMEA countries on trade with the West. In particular, the Soviet Union has a lower level of engagement in foreign trade as a whole than do most Western industrialized countries. The share of all foreign merchandise trade in the Soviet gross national product appears to have consistently been in the range of 5 percent (total published exports plus imports divided by two as a percentage of GNP).[1] The corresponding share of foreign trade to GNP in West Germany, on the other hand, has generally exceeded 20 percent. However, the actual share of East-West trade in the national product of the Soviet Union and the Western European countries is, in both cases, quite low. In the Soviet Union's case, East-West trade as a percentage of GNP in 1979 was 1.3 percent; in the case of most Western industrialized countries it ranged up to 1.5 percent at the most.[2] For the Eastern European countries, whose economies are much more dependent on trade than is the Soviet Union's, East-West trade by itself has a somewhat greater significance, ranging from just over 2 percent of GNP in Bulgaria and Czechoslovakia to 5 percent in Romania.

C. FINANCING THE GROWTH OF TRADE

Throughout the period of rapid growth in trade, the CMEA countries had substantial balance of trade deficits with the Western countries. Starting with a relatively modest trade deficit of $0.1 billion in 1970 (which included a Polish and a Soviet surplus), the CMEA countries reached a peak annual deficit of $8.0 billion in 1975 (Exhibit 5). Their plans had been to reach a turnaround by that time, relying on added production by the credit-financed installations to provide increased exports to the West. Instead the deficits persisted, compelling the Eastern European countries to control their imports more rigorously. Despite a reversal in the trend of the trade deficits, however, the demand for hard currency to meet ever-increasing interest payments created a spiraling need for injections of new debt. The result is shown in Exhibit 6. The net hard currency indebtedness of Eastern Europe rose from an estimated $19 billion at the end of 1975 to almost $56 billion at the end of 1980 — a compound annual rate of growth of 24 percent, at a time when merchandise imports were growing at only a 10 percent annual rate.[3] The net debt of the Soviet Union grew more slowly, reaching $10.4 billion in 1980. While debt levels were rising rapidly through the '70s, the relative stagnation of CMEA exports meant that the ratio of outstanding debt to annual exports expanded dramatically

---

[1]The National Foreign Assessment Center of the CIA estimates that the figure is actually closer to 8 percent. Other sources suggest that the figure may be higher still, arguing that barter and artificial pricing tend to cause Soviet ruble trade to be understated.

[2]This does not include Austria (3.2 percent) and Finland (7.1 percent).

[3]Net indebtedness is calculated as the total of all outstanding debts of the CMEA countries (gross indebtedness) less hard currency deposits in Western banks. Gross indebtedness of the CMEA is estimated at $80.3 billion as of the end of 1980.

Exhibit 5
CMEA Trade Deficits with the OECD
1970-1981

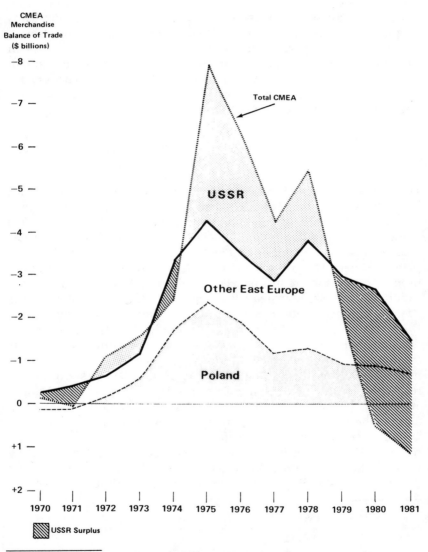

CMEA
Merchandise
Balance of Trade
($ billions)

Total CMEA

USSR

Other East Europe

Poland

USSR Surplus

Note: Deficits understated by FOB export valuation of Western goods.
Source: OECD, *Statistics of Foreign Trade, Series A*

Exhibit 6

OUTSTANDING CMEA DEBT
1971-1980
(net hard currency debt in $ billion)

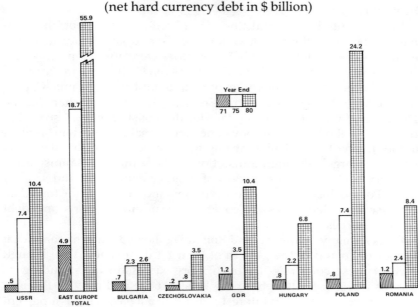

Source: US Dept of Commerce; CIA
* Net Hard Currency Debt in $ Billion

for most CMEA countries from 1972 to 1979, resulting in an increasingly heavy debt service burden.

After 1975, the Soviet Union and Poland, which together accounted for 75 percent of the CMEA deficit in 1975, substantially reduced their trade deficits (Exhibit 5). The Soviet Union accomplished this mainly by diverting increasing amounts of its energy resources to the West and enjoying the higher world prices of oil. Poland, on the other hand, reduced its trade deficit mainly by slowing the growth of its imports. The difference in performance between the Soviet and Polish economies — no doubt at least partly as a result of these alternate strategies — is striking. From 1975 to 1980, the Soviet economy continued to grow at a real rate of about 2.7 percent per year, moderately under the 1970-75 pace of 3.7 percent. Poland, however, had been growing at 6.6 percent per year in real terms from 1970 to 1975, faster than any other member of the CMEA. But after 1975, while borrowing from the West soared, growth slowed sharply, turning negative in 1980. Thus, Poland had an

23

average real growth of less than 1 percent between 1975 and 1980.[1] To be sure, that was not solely due to the squeeze put on imports of hard currency goods. Economic stagnation was also exacerbated by the inefficient use made of many imports and by the labor unrest created by political problems.

In analyzing the accumulation of net hard currency debt, the comparison between the Soviet Union and Poland is significant. In the early '70s, the debt levels of both countries were approximately equal (Exhibit 6). Indeed in 1972 Poland looked even healthier than the Soviet Union in terms of its debt-to-export ratio, and through much of the decade the Soviets ran larger trade deficits with the West than did the Poles. Yet, by the end of the decade, the Polish debt had soared to nearly $25 billion, while the Soviet net debt remained less than half that amount. The Soviet Union seems to have been able to balance its payments largely through transactions outside the merchandise trade category such as increased sales of military equipment and sales of gold. Poland has not had these options and so has been forced to increase its indebtedness to cover its continuing imports and debt service charges.

East Germany, Hungary, and Romania followed patterns somewhat similar to Poland in the growth of their hard currency debt, though each of these countries has been more successful in expanding its exports along with its debt to the West. At the end of 1979, Poland's debt service ratio (i.e., its interest plus principal payments as a percent of hard currency exports) was 92 percent compared with East Germany's 54 percent, Hungary's 37 percent, and Romania's 22 percent. As of June 1980, it is estimated that 37 percent of the gross debt of the CMEA countries to the West was due within one year; only 43 percent of the debt had a maturity beyond two years.[2] The declining average maturity of these debts has the effect, of course, of increasing the annual debt service obligation. As a result, severe pressure has already been put on the hard currency reserves of all the CMEA countries. From mid-1980 to mid-1981, moreover, the aggregate deposits of CMEA countries in Western banks dropped sharply as they liquidated assets not only to meet interest and maturity requirements, but also to pay for imports and avoid seeking additional loans.

Most of the drop in CMEA reserves in the first half of 1981 was accounted for by the Soviet Union. Disbursements to support Poland during the early phases of its debt service crisis were accompanied by a

---

[1] Since 1980, the Polish economy appears to have declined in real terms by possibly 20 percent.
[2] The BIS provides data on indebtedness to banks showing that as of July 1981 the USSR had $6.81 billion due within one year; Poland, $4.7; East Germany, $4.0; Hungary, $2.5; Romania, $2.3; Czechoslovakia, $1.2; and Bulgaria, $0.9.

$1.0 billion trade deficit with the OECD countries. That deficit was reversed during the second half of 1981, however. Soviet imports were sharply curtailed and, as Exhibit 5 shows, the USSR ended the year with a $2.6 billion trade surplus with the OECD.[1] In addition, Soviet gold sales during 1981 are estimated to have been about $2.5 billion.

The creditors of the CMEA countries consist of banks, exporters who extend trade credit, and governments which both guarantee bank loans and make some loans directly. At the end of 1980, the gross debt of the CMEA countries to all categories of lenders in the West was $81.4 billion; after offsetting balances of $15.1 billion with Western banks and others, the net debt was the $66.3 billion shown in Exhibit 6. Data on the distribution of the debt among types of lenders are available only for the gross amounts. These indicate that at the end of 1980 most of the government-backed debt (largely in various forms of guarantees) had been extended to Poland ($10.1 billion) and the USSR ($8.2 billion). Because of the size and significance of the Soviet and Polish markets, these two countries have been particularly attractive targets for Western exports.[2] The particular problems of the Polish debt in 1982 are discussed further in Section II, Part E. The aggregate of gross debt to the other five CMEA countries that is backed by Western governments was $3.1 billion at the end of 1980. Given the likelihood of continued low export earnings, the existing debts will presumably have to be refinanced, and at higher interest rates.

D. GROWTH AND INVESTMENT IN THE CMEA

The ability of the socialist countries of the CMEA to grow and to improve their standards of living is crucially dependent, as it is in the West, upon improving productivity. Since the nature of the planning process in some of the socialist systems has impaired labor initiative, there is substantial room in all of them for productivity improvement through increasing the incentives and improving the skills of the labor force. In addition, of course, much of any gain must depend upon improving the quality and design of the capital goods in use on the farms and in the factories and upon more efficient allocation of resources among alternative uses. Even though voluntary or forced

[1]Based on preliminary data in OECD, *Statistics of Foreign Trade, Series A,* May 1982. No data were available for this period on Soviet trade in services, nor for hard currency trade with non-OECD countries.

[2]Soviet GNP is estimated to be about 2.5 times the size of Eastern Europe's as a whole. The Soviet population is about 2.4 times that of Eastern Europe making per capita GNP slightly higher on average. Poland contains about 32 percent of the Eastern European population and about the same proportion of its GNP. International Bank for Reconstruction and Development, *World Development Report, 1981* (Washington: 1981), p. 135 (Table 1).

savings have been large enough to have added an adequate stock of new capital goods, the investment base has not produced the growth in output needed to meet targets, presumably for reasons of both technical and managerial inefficiency. Consequently, although nominal investment is rather high in most socialist economies, the real value of the additional capital actually installed, to the extent that it can be measured by the present value of the future income streams flowing from the investment, must clearly be rather low.

The discouragement over this entire process is well expressed by a Czech economist:

> It is becoming clear that for a full thirty years we have been unable to solve problems associated with production under socialism, either in theory or in practice.[1]

Insofar as the deficiencies are attributable to inefficient or poorly deployed equipment, the adjustments necessary to increase productivity can be accomplished with the least strain if there is a growing supply of domestic saving out of current incomes and an increasing supply of domestically produced capital goods. In general, the problem in the Eastern countries is that even though they succeed in creating enough savings, either through voluntary or compulsory means, they lack the capacity to produce domestically the variety and quality of investment goods needed to gain an optimum position — in terms of product mix and productive efficiency — for meeting their growth targets and to produce a significant volume of exports competitive on world markets. Consequently, the Eastern countries, following the traditional pattern for economic development throughout the world, have added to their capital investment by borrowing funds and importing capital equipment from other countries. So long as they could defer repayment, and meet their interest payments abroad with other current export earnings, they could presumably have time enough to bring their new tools into production without serious domestic disruption. In an ideal situation, the added output could eventually support sufficient exports of acceptable quality to earn abroad the funds needed to service the debt, with enough left over to enlarge real incomes at home.

The debt problems that emerged in 1981 arose, however, because some of the resources that had been borrowed by the CMEA countries had either been spent on consumer goods, presumably with the aim of improving labor's performance, or used to purchase assets that were subsequently less productive than hoped. By 1980, some current

---

[1]From an article by Jarowlav Vejvoda published in Prague in October 1981 and quoted in *The New York Times*, "As Poland's Economy Slides, Comecon Feels the Backlash," January 10, 1982, p. E4.

borrowings had to be used merely to meet the interest costs on previous credits; meanwhile the scope for additional borrowing in the West was shrinking. As a consequence, capital building in the 'eighties may have to be carried out largely with internally generated savings. Yet in the USSR, and in varying degrees among the East European countries, a substantial portion of domestic savings is already absorbed in supporting the bureaucratic structure of the planned economy and in paying the cost of Warsaw Pact military expenditures. Although estimates vary, the Warsaw Pact countries appear to spend from 8 to 13 percent of their GNP on military expenditures, or two to three times the proportion spent in the NATO countries.[1] The USSR appears to allocate resources to its military program with a stern priority, leaving the civilian sector in a residual position with respect to sharing in the available supply of goods and services.

The socialist economic policies of most CMEA countries preclude another source of capital, namely equity investment from the West, although certain types of compensatory financing arrangements have a rough correspondence to the risk profile of equity participation (to be discussed further in Section II, below). Conversely, the Soviet Union and other CMEA members, while importing borrowed capital, have not been able to afford to invest capital abroad as a source of future earnings. They prefer to limit their disbursements abroad to the support of trading offices and modest trade credits. Any other external credits (as well as military assistance) appear to be extended mainly for political motives, such as the support of Cuba, or Ethiopia, and are intermingled with subsidies through outright grants or the purchase of goods at artificially high prices. Such disbursements, rather than adding appreciably to external earnings, appear to be a considerable net drain on whatever export earnings the Soviet Union or other CMEA countries may have. Unless such drains diminish, or other sizable sources of export earnings are developed, the prospect would seem to be that any renewal of expanding economic relations, if that should be possible after the current political strains have lessened, would depend on the availability of further credits from the West. Indeed such credits may be necessary even to maintain the current levels of trade.

Partly as a result of difficulties in the formation of a stock of productive capital, the CMEA countries have all fallen behind their Five-Year Plan targets for 1976-80, and have subsequently reduced their targets for 1981-85. With the possible exception of Hungary, the Eastern

[1]Ruth Leger Sivard, *World Military and Social Expenditures, 1981* (Leesburg, Va.: World Priorities, 1981). Estimates for Soviet expenditure range from about 11 percent by the Stockholm International Peace Research Institute (SIPRI) to over 16 percent by the CIA, compared to the reported U.S. expenditures of 5.1 percent of GNP.

Exhibit 7

ANNUAL REAL GNP GROWTH IN CMEA COUNTRIES*
1965-1980
(percent annual growth rate**)

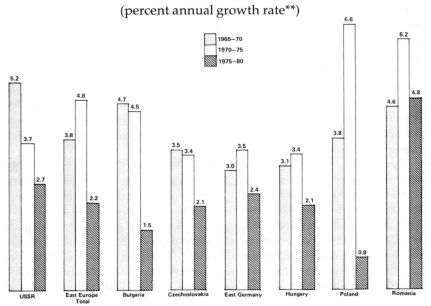

* Figures represent sources' estimation of GNP to conform with Western conventions. Official national statistics of the CMEA countries are generally higher. For example, the USSR reports that its "Produced National Income" grew at a 5.7% rate in 1970-75, and a 4.1% rate in 1975-80, as opposed to the 3.7% and 2.7% charted above for the same respective periods.

** Calculated as a least squares trend.

Sources: National Foreign Assessment Center, CIA, *Handbook of Economic Statistics, 1981* (Washington: CIA, 1981)

European countries have been caught in a vicious circle. They need rising incomes as a source of the savings required for domestic capital formation; yet they did not get a sufficient rise in incomes out of past capital formation to make it possible for domestic belt-tightening to yield the needed additions to capital formation (without so reducing consumption as to create social unrest). Exhibit 7 shows the pattern of GNP growth in the CMEA countries over the 1965-80 period.

Only the USSR reached its target for gross fixed investment in 1976-80, and all of the CMEA countries fell short of their targets for growth in national production, including both industrial and agricultural output.[1] Overall, according to published CMEA statistics,

[1]German Institute for Economic Research, "The CMEA Countries' Problematic Plan Targets," *Economic Bulletin*, Sept. 1981, pp. 3-13.

"produced national income" grew at an annual rate of 4.0 percent from 1975 through 1980, well under the target range of 5.8 to 6.1 percent. (To be sure, this compares to a 3.0 percent rate for real GNP growth in the West as stagflation spread; but as the Western countries have already achieved much higher per capita income levels, most of them can carve out of those incomes enough savings to make reasonably adequate provision for current investment without reducing current consumption.) The CMEA countries have recently scaled back their targets for 1981 to 1985 to a range of 3.6 to 3.9 percent annual growth in output.

Meanwhile, Romania and Poland have begun to experience the backlash of having borrowed heavily abroad without sufficiently increasing real productivity at home to produce growing incomes and growing exports to service the debt. The future implications of the current financial position are discussed further in Section II, Part E.

E. RECENT DEVELOPMENTS:
IMPLICATIONS FOR TRILATERAL ACTION

The remarkable expansion of East-West trade persisted during the 'seventies because the opening of economic opportunities exerted a compelling attraction, and political differences were confined to skirmishes of diplomacy. But Soviet entry into Afghanistan at the end of the decade broke the spell of mild euphoria, and in the United States, most notably, the two tracks of political and economic action came together. The always latent political (and ideological) wariness of the West became a dominant force. At the same time, in sharp contrast with the beginning of the 'seventies when recession promoted the expansion of trade with the East, the worldwide economic sluggishness of 1981 had a dampening influence. With respect to Eastern Europe this aggravated, and was in turn aggravated by, the signs of impending problems of debt service for Poland and Romania. The ready availability of Western credits, on which a part of the Western exports had been floated, began to dry up — even before Poland's resort to martial law at the end of 1981.

Throughout 1980 the United States was also urging the other leading industrial countries of the West to impose economic sanctions on the Soviet Union as a penalizing demonstration of Western disapproval of the Soviet action in Afghanistan. The rather spotty response to this urging in the West, and the obvious failure to achieve an impact on the Soviet behavior in Afghanistan, have not deterred new calls for sanctions against both the USSR and Poland in 1982 to encourage the Polish Government to change course: to revoke martial law, to recognize and take into its councils the Solidarity Union, and to free the Union's

29

imprisoned members. Whether or not further sanctions, or "signals" (the more modest form initiated by the United Kingdom), may be imposed, the clear initial effect — in conjunction with continuing recession in 1982 in the West — is to prevent any widespread resumption of East-West trade expansion for some time. Indeed this might be one of the reasons, though certainly not the most important one, why the Five-Year Plans of most of the CMEA countries contemplate a decline in total imports from the West, particularly in the category of machinery and transportation equipment.

This does not mean a general shutdown of trade, however. Hungary achieved a balanced two-way trade with the West in 1980 and 1981, partly through an effective domestic belt-tightening program to hold per capita consumption constant while releasing more home production both for export and for tooling up in order to expand production and external trade in 1982 and beyond. Bulgaria on a lower per capita scale has pursued a similarly effective plan for home production and for sustained, and possibly increasing, trade with the West. Czechoslovakia, if able to overcome some disorder in the internal flow of materials and the utilization of capacity, may in time become a more active trading partner with the West, partly because her external borrowing thus far has been comparatively modest.

Trade between the two Germanys will also remain substantial. The development of intra-German trade has been encouraged by special arrangements between the two countries. This includes an agreement by West Germany to finance the "swing" in any bilateral trade at a zero rate of interest, thus encouraging imports by the GDR. Moreover, no customs duties are levied. These concessionary terms also lead to an onward flow of East German goods, once inside the sheltered market of the European Economic Community, to other countries in the Community. That artificial stimulus for East German exports to the West may in time be modified because of complaints from other members of the EEC.[1] At present, intra-German trade is approximately balanced, with the GDR showing a slight surplus in 1981 on a turnover of DM 12.5 billion.[2]

The Soviet Union because of her size and diversity is inevitably a special case. She has become primarily an importer and exporter of raw materials — grains and energy — and just the converse of the United

---

[1] Horst Lambrecht, "Entwicklung der Wirtschaftsbeziehungen zur Bundesrepublik Deutschland," *Drei Jahrzehnte Aussenpolitik der DDR*, Eberhard Schulz et al., eds., (München: 1979).
[2] Horst Lambrecht, "Innerdeutscher Handel,"*DDR und Osteuropa, Ein Handbuch*, (Opladen: 1981), p. 161.

States, which is an exporter of grain and an importer of energy. It is with respect to recent developments affecting future trading possibilities with the Soviet Union that more needs to be said here in overall terms, before turning in Section II to the detailed prospects and problems in particular economic sectors, and in Section III to the range of policy options that will confront the West over the longer term.

The USSR deserves a closer look not only because of 1) the sanctions which have been imposed on her trade since early 1980, and because of 2) her plans for exporting more natural gas to Western Europe, but also because of 3) provisions of the Eleventh Five-Year Plan (1981-85) which affect the functioning of her entire economy and its relation to trade with the West.

Sanctions[1]

The principal restrictive sanction in 1980 was the partial embargo by the United States of agricultural exports to the Soviet Union. The minimum assured amount under the terms of a 1975 grain supply agreement, 8 million metric tons, was still supplied; but contracts for an additional 14 million metric tons (valued in total at more than $2 billion), and negotiations for another 3 million, were canceled.

With some delay, and inconvenience, the Soviet Union replaced from other foreign sources all but an estimated 2.5 million metric tons of the embargoed U.S. grain shipments. In effect, it gained another 1.5 million metric tons by reducing its own shipments to Eastern Europe as the United States increased its sales to those countries. The Soviet Union has subsequently established longer term buying arrangements with several of the alternate suppliers which it used to offset its shortfall. The U.S. grain traders in turn were able to sell some of their excess grain to markets that had previously been served by the countries which in 1980 shifted their exports to fill the USSR deficiency. Nonetheless, during the 1979/80 grain year the Commodity Credit Corporation and other U.S. governmental agencies attempted to insulate U.S. markets from the shock of the suspension. They assumed the contractual obligations of the grain companies for a total of more than 14 million metric tons cf wheat, corn, and soybeans that had been pre-

---

[1]Most data concerning sanctions have been taken from *An Assessment of the Afghanistan Sanctions: Implications for Trade and Diplomacy in the 1980s*, a report prepared for the Subcommittee on Europe and the Middle East of the Committee on Foreign Affairs, U.S. House of Representatives, by the Office of Senior Specialists, Congressional Research Service, Library of Congress (Washington, D.C.: U.S. Government Printing Office, April 1981), a 133-page study. Other aspects of the sanctions as they applied to agricultural products are discussed further in Section II, Part B, below.

viously committed for export to the USSR. The resulting domestic budgetary cost was about $2.5 billion, with a corresponding loss in the balance of payments.[1]

Although President Carter in December 1980 extended the grain embargo and other export controls for another year, President Reagan, having made a campaign pledge to lift the embargo, did so in April 1981. Other U.S. sanctions imposed in 1980 and still continuing in 1982 placed new limits on fishing rights, aircraft landing rights, and private as well as official exchanges of a commercial, scientific, or cultural nature. Tighter standards have also been applied by the United States to industrial exports containing high technology, supplementing the CoCom proscriptions described in Section III; but most actual curtailments have been readily replaced by other Western suppliers. One result of the experience thus far with sanctions imposed by the West has been to persuade the USSR, albeit at some expense and diffusion of effort, to seek out alternative suppliers for any imported goods in order to obtain the protection of diversification, meanwhile reducing the United States to a position of residual rather than primary supplier.

Natural Gas and the Pipeline

The issues of dependence and diversification are reversed in the case of the proposed enlargement of Soviet deliveries of natural gas to Western Europe. Concern over the risks of possible Soviet attempts at leverage is not idle speculation, because the Soviet Union has in the past for various reasons cut down its supply of energy to various countries. In 1979 and 1981, because of cold weather and other supply disruptions, it reduced flows of natural gas to West Germany and Austria at times by as much as 50 percent. It has also tried to exert leverage for political reasons, at different times cutting the supply of oil to Yugoslavia, Finland, China, and Israel, and perhaps on occasions even to Poland, as an expression of Soviet displeasure.[2]

By 1981 the Soviet Union was providing about 15 percent of the combined natural gas requirements of all of Western Europe. This created an encouraging environment in which to conclude negotiations begun in the late 'seventies for a further doubling in the proportion of the USSR contribution to Western Europe's growing gas consumption by 1984 or 1985. The new supply, some 40 billion cubic

---

[1]Roughly $2.0 billion of this total was subsequently recovered in resales of these contracts; but estimates of other indirect losses of revenue by the Treasury nearly offset that $2.0 billion direct recovery.

[2]Marshall I. Goldman, "Energy Prospects for The Soviet Union and Eastern Europe," November 1981, a paper prepared for private circulation.

meters, is to come through a new pipeline complex from the Urengoi field in northwestern Siberia. To be sure, the USSR would need equipment and supplies for the construction and operation of the new pipeline. Her own capacity, though growing, could not handle the vast requirements for production of the pipe itself, the heavy machinery for pipe-laying, or the forty or more compressor stations needed to keep the gas flowing at full capacity through the pipeline once installed. This seemed a natural opportunity for two-way trade, with much of the needed material coming from the West and financed by Western banks until repayment could be made in effect by delivery of the gas. Eventually, in addition to the gas sales needed for the repayments, more gas would be left over for the Soviet Union to sell for hard currency which she could use to make more purchases (possibly even American grain) in the West.

Problems arose when the United States, very sensitive to opportunities for either side to use economic leverage for political ends, became concerned that a heavy dependence by Western Europe on vital energy from the USSR could open up three risks: 1) that the USSR could earn enough hard currency to be able to buy technology or materials that would dangerously strengthen the economic base for her military potential; or 2) that the USSR could tighten the valve on the flow of gas at crucial times to exert powerful political leverage on Western Europe; or 3) that the USSR could cripple Western Europe's ability to resist by terminating supplies in case of actual warfare.

The result of the U.S. opposition to the new pipeline has been to increase serious friction within the Western alliance at a time when economic malaise had already been aggravated by strains emanating from high U.S. interest rates and the concomitant depreciation of Western currencies against the U.S. dollar — adding to upward cost pressures in Europe, Canada, and Japan, as the domestic prices of all imports rose, most notably imported energy. The general view in Western Europe in contrast with the official position of the United States Government is: 1) that Soviet gas offers a useful further diversification of energy sources, potentially reducing dependence on OPEC oil; 2) that the proportion of dependence on Soviet gas will still be moderate (except perhaps for Italy, although she is negotiating for additional supplies from North Africa); 3) that adequate contingency plans are being prepared to use the existing natural gas grid in the event of an interruption of Soviet supplies (regardless of whether the interruption should be caused by a natural disaster or a malevolent Soviet act); and 4) that the USSR will be at least as dependent on the hard currency earnings from the gas as Western Europe would be dependent on the gas deliveries. Moreover, some Western Europeans add, the knowledge by the USSR that comprehensive (if costly) backup capacity is available will reduce the likelihood that the USSR would attempt to use control over the gas supply as leverage to achieve political influence.

Nonetheless, the United States has continued vigorous opposition. Having concentrated for a time on urging such alternatives to Soviet gas as sales of American coal, the United States found its case weakened when Europeans pointed out that such alternatives would be welcome additions to the contingency reserves which they must have, but need not be used while the Soviet gas was available. To that the United States has responded by attempting to impede progress on the pipeline through embargoing U.S. supplier components, and components from U.S. licensees in Europe, for any part of the project. The practical results may be to slow down the pipeline construction as components are ordered and produced elsewhere, but the more serious consequence is the divisive impact on the Western alliance and the clearly demonstrated need for development of a policy consensus among the Trilateral countries on the relations between political and trade objectives — including the possible future use of sanctions, an objective toward which Section III is directed.

The Eleventh Five-Year Plan[1]
The Soviet Plan published in March 1981 has had to cope with a dilemma that became increasingly sharp during the later 'seventies: the conflict between a persistent slowdown in economic growth, characterized by a sharp deterioration in performance, and the clearly related need to increase work incentives by making more consumer goods available. Support of the military establishment just as clearly had preempted resources that might otherwise have been converted to the raising of living standards. Recognizing that the Soviet Union's slower growth will limit availabilities for new investment, the Plan only allows for an average annual growth in investments of 2.1 percent. Yet it looks for an overall annual growth of national output by 3.4 percent. Given this rate of investment growth, and the reduced growth rate of the Soviet labor force, such a rise of output implies an average annual growth of man-hour productivity, as well as increases in investment from outside the current Plan. That is, as explained by Soviet officials,

---

[1]This review of the Eleventh Plan draws heavily on *The Soviet Five-Year Plan (1981-85)*, an unpublished monograph by John P. Hardt and Kate S. Tomlinson of the Congressional Research Service, Library of Congress.

34

large capital projects initiated and largely paid for in the previous planning period will come into production after relatively little further outlays during the current five-year period.

Increased worker productivity will depend, to an important extent, on higher living standards, which in turn imply continued growth of grain and meat production. In effect, after three years of nearly disastrous harvests attributed to bad weather (and a fourth bad year appearing likely as of mid-'82), the Plan forecasts five good years, with particular attention to improved storage and transportation to avoid losses and spoilage of crops once grown. But there is also an expectation of continued grain imports, as well as imports of technology to raise farm and transport efficiency. Indeed, imports of technology and credit will apparently provide significant marginal elements in the targets which the Plan contemplates for the priority sectors of energy, agricultural and transport equipment, petrochemicals and chemicals, and computers. While the total magnitude of planned imports may not rise appreciably above the total in 1980,[1] any substantial absolute declines would probably jeopardize the target for planned increases in output over the 1981-85 period.

---

[1]USSR data indicate a figure of about 11.0 billion rubles for imports in 1980 from the seven "Summit" countries — Canada, France, Italy, Japan, the United Kingdom, the United States, and West Germany.

II.   Potentials and Problems in Key Economic Sectors

After World War II, the Japanese developed a philosophy of proceeding on two tracks —political and economic — as quite distinct routes in their dealings with the communist countries, particularly with China. But even in their relations with the USSR, despite strong political differences highlighted by contention over the four northern islands, the Japanese and the Soviets were able to find a common interest in major projects in Siberia. Those special activities along with other commercial trade gave the USSR a trade surplus with Japan, but were also sufficient to make Japan the leading Western trading partner (i.e., exports plus imports) of the USSR until 1972 when West Germany took over the leadership because of her rapid expansion of exports to the USSR. But late in the '70s, even though she had negotiated several major projects with the USSR in the mid-'70s, Japan found more difficulty in keeping economic and political issues separate. And by the '80s, any evaluation of the economic potentials for USSR-Japan trade, just as for all trade between the two vast markets of the CMEA and the Trilateral countries, has had to balance prospective economic gains against the political or strategic exposure in the relationship.

The operational word, however, is "balance." Economic relations cannot be sealed off completely in an effort to establish a political polarity; instead a kind of centripetal force is continually at work drawing natural trading areas into relations with each other. Some trading and financial relations are too attractive to both sides for them to be completely cut off. Consequently, the question facing the Trilateral governments, and no doubt those of the CMEA countries as well, is how far to encourage or permit economic relations to go — that is, how to weigh the flow of benefits from many kinds of economic exchange against the possibility that they might also weaken a country's strategic position. Each key sector to be discussed here has been reviewed with a focus on those aspects which may imply some degree of economic vulnerability for the West, as well as some risk of creating conflicts among the Western countries. In many cases, as already suggested, limits on interdependence are set by the sheer difficulty of doing business with the bureaucracies of the centrally planned countries. The problems of policy arise when these operational barriers are overcome and considerations of national interest have to be applied. A suggested general approach to the national security interests of the Trilateral countries in those circumstances is outlined in Section III.

In this section the specific potentials and risks in five sectors of East-West economic activity are considered: (A) energy, in which the main flow of trade is from East to West; (B) agriculture, in which the direction of trade flow presently is mainly from West to East; (C) technology and its application in manufacturing and mining, in which the trade is two-way, but presently tilted on balance from West to East; (D) services, which the Eastern countries are aggressively promoting; and (E) finance, in which the net flow has been from West to East, and will probably remain so, although on a reduced scale and with stricter limits on credit availability for some time to come. Indeed, credit is currently the economic obstacle most likely to limit any otherwise potentially desirable expansion of trade and investment in the years immediately ahead.

A. ENERGY

Present Dependence on USSR Energy

Energy from the Soviet Union provides a relatively small proportion of Western Europe's requirements in contrast with the relative importance of Soviet energy deliveries to the CMEA group. Except for Poland, traditionally a net exporter of coal, the proportions of primary energy dependence on the USSR by the CMEA countries in 1978 ranged from one-quarter (East Germany) to two-thirds (Bulgaria). By contrast, the larger industrialized countries of Western Europe consumed primary energy from the USSR in proportions that ranged in 1980 from less than 0.2 percent of total requirements in the United Kingdom (before North Sea oil it was 3.1 percent) to 7.5 percent in Italy.[1] Coal from Poland has been the only other significant source of energy in the West from the CMEA group, until recent cutbacks. While important because of its quality for particular uses, and important to Poland because of the foreign exchange it can earn, the actual volume of coal imports from Poland has been a relatively negligible percentage in

---

[1]Data for gas imports alone indicate, however, that among smaller countries, imports from the USSR represent 9.7 percent of Austria's primary energy consumption, and 3.6 percent of Finland's. *Petroleum Economist*, August 1981, p. 337; *BP Statistical Review of the World Oil Industry*, 1980, p.16.

the total energy consumption of any of the countries in Western Europe for which data are available.

Viewed from the Soviet side, however, energy plays a critical role in its trade with the Western industrial countries. In 1979, the USSR earned 68 percent of its total foreign exchange from energy exports to the OECD countries; of this, 58 percent in that year came from exports of oil. Flows of natural gas are becoming more important in the '80s. The export of the Soviet Union's gas is expected to gradually replace its oil, paralleling the changing composition of energy production in the USSR and the shift underway there from the use of oil as energy to its domestic use as a feedstock for petrochemicals. Preliminary data for 1981 show that oil exports have fallen in real terms and as a proportion of exports, while natural gas has expanded to 13 percent of total Soviet exports.[1] The Eleventh Plan projects a rise of only 3 to 5 percent in 1985 over the 1980 production of oil, well below the planned overall growth in Soviet national production, while a rise of 38 to 48 percent is foreseen over the same period in gas production.

The Urengoi Pipeline

The extent to which the sizable expansion of gas production in northwestern Siberia will become available to the countries of Western Europe, after set-asides for Soviet and other CMEA requirements, depends on the completion of plans for the controversial pipeline from the Urengoi field. For the most part, contracts for the first stage of construction have already been signed with firms in the West to provide for deliveries of the needed steel pipe, pipe layers, and compressors; much of the related financing has been arranged; and delivery contracts for the gas have been or are being negotiated with companies in West Germany, France, the Netherlands, Belgium, Italy, Austria, and Switzerland.

The United States Government, as already mentioned, has blocked the sale of some pipeline components by U.S. firms, but there is as yet no evidence that this action will seriously delay completion of the project in 1984 or 1985. If present schedules are fulfilled, by 1985 total gas imports by West European countries from all sources in the Soviet Union will represent the following percentages of estimated primary energy consumption at that time: France, 3.8 (vs. 1.2 in 1980); the Netherlands, 4.3; West Germany, 5.9 (vs. 3.3); Belgium-Luxembourg,

---

[1]Data on Soviet oil and gas exports from John P. Hardt, Congressional Research Service, Washington, D.C.

6.8; and Italy, 7.5 (vs. 4.1).[1] Overall deliveries of Soviet gas are expected to increase from 25 billion cubic meters in 1981 to about 65 bcm in 1985, as Soviet oil deliveries shrink but Western energy requirements rise. Meanwhile, consumption of natural gas, both imported and domestic, by the members of the International Energy Agency as a group (plus France), is expected to decline slightly as a proportion of total primary energy consumption — from 19.5 percent in 1979 to 18.3 percent in 1990, suggesting that Europe is not committed to a major expansion of its dependence on gas as a source of energy.

No doubt a total cut-off of the expected gas deliveries from the USSR would require a major re-allocation of energy within Western Europe. But the impact would be less severe proportionally than that exerted by the curtailment of OPEC oil supplies in 1973, when the remaining energy available in Western European countries was nonetheless re-allocated adequately to the priority sectors in each country. In any event, there need be no more than a brief pause for re-arrangement if the USSR supplies of natural gas should be interrupted or curtailed for any reason, because plans are well prepared to draw on other sources which could soon make up for any overall shortfall, though perhaps at some increase in cost.

Some increased supplies of oil and possibly gas would presumably be available from OPEC or other oil and gas exporting countries. Contingency arrangements for coal supplies from the United States, Australia, or other major coal producers are already being considered. Indeed, according to United States officials, coal could replace at any time the additional energy expected to arrive through the new gas pipeline starting in 1984 or 1985. The already existing West European Natural Gas Agreement among the principal users, which also includes such user-suppliers as the Netherlands and Norway (though unfortunately the United Kingdom has not yet agreed to participate), is capable of providing through the "grid" a mutual safety net, immediately available for all participants if an interruption should occur. Over a short period of only a few weeks, by drawing on existing reserve capacity, the Agreement could offset a total interruption of the gas supply from the USSR while alternate sources of gas were being activated, and utilities and industry switched to the use of substitute fuels. This switchover capability is already widely installed.

Consideration of the stake of Western European countries in this pipeline, being built exclusively to serve them, should not neglect the

[1]*Petroleum Economist*, "Foreign Trade Statistics," August 1981, p. 356; Presse- und Informationsamt der Bundesregierung, *Aktuelle Beiträge zur Wirtschafts- und Finanzpolitik*, Nr. 55/1981, pp. 17-24.

Soviet stake. The Soviet Union will have invested the equivalent of $5 to $6 billion of hard currency, plus substantial domestic resources, in the total project. In addition, after payments for the imported pipeline equipment, the Soviet Union will earn $7 to $10 billion annually in current (i.e., 1985 and beyond) dollars from expected gas exports. The USSR can use these proceeds to help meet any other deficit in its trade with the West, or to provide resources for the CMEA through the IBEC or the IIB, or to service outstanding debt. Rather than dramatically increasing Soviet hard currency earnings later in the '80s, as U.S. officials seem to fear, the income from gas sales will probably be only barely sufficient to offset the reduction of earnings resulting from declining oil exports. In real terms, Soviet hard currency income from all energy exports may actually be lower in 1990 than the $16 to $17 billion of peak earnings reached in 1980 and 1981. Gas sales through the pipelines appear to provide the Soviets the best, and perhaps the only, means of sustaining the level of real imports from the West prevailing in the early '80s.

This means that the cost to the USSR would be high if it were to curtail the gas delivered through the proposed new pipeline as a lever for exacting political or strategic concessions from Western Europe. The loss of foreign exchange and the economic cost of idling the new or existing pipelines would be substantial, not to mention the possible impact of Western retaliation, while the leverage would be minimal because of the relatively small part which Soviet gas would play in the total diversified energy requirements of the West.

Prospective Energy Development
Perhaps the significance of the pipeline has been overblown. While unfortunately creating acrimonious disagreement between the United States and its Western European allies, it has, nonetheless, served to bring forward for more serious consideration a broader issue: Given the tendency of a growing world to undergo repeated experiences of energy shortage, to what extent should the Trilateral countries actively support the development of other potential sources of energy everywhere, including the Soviet Union, on the ground that most forms of energy are fungible and that any increase in energy-producing capacity is desirable, wherever it may occur?

In the context of the pipeline dispute, which has centered on the dependent position of West European users of energy, the issue might be resolved by simply recognizing the need to keep supplies diversified and contingency plans active for coping with a possible curtailment of any one source. This is indeed a precept which presumably

40

guides any well-run utility firm engaged in supplying energy. Is there a serious risk, however, that additional sales of oil and gas production equipment to the Soviet Union will, in the end, simply enable it to become so amply self-sufficient in energy that it can embark on aggrandizing world adventure with abandon? Or, taking a different view, is it more likely that by contributing to greater energy development within the Soviet Union, the West can reduce the risks it now fears of any Soviet incursion into the Middle East that might be aimed at insuring the availability of oil and gas to the USSR?

These various interpretations reflect the West's perpetual dilemma in defining the political and strategic relationship between the Trilateral countries and the USSR. Does the Soviet Union really seek world domination or does it instead simply seek a stand-off in the great power relationship? While statesmen vacillate over that dilemma, various countries in the West take different approaches to the specific opportunities in the energy field. Energy specialists generally agree that, with regard to energy, the supposed dilemma is largely irrelevant. In all likelihood, the Soviet Union, even if left to rely only on its own production and distribution capabilities, will be able to remain self-sufficient in energy for decades to come, albeit with a changing mix of energy sources, and despite continued exports to its Eastern European partners. Some of any further oil or gas production increases would probably, however, be accomplished more readily by importing additional equipment or technology from the West. And there are a number of possibilities for both sides to undertake successful cooperation, to that end, if governments agree.

For example, during the visit of President Brezhnev to West Germany in November 1981, long-term plans were discussed concerning projects for refining sulfurous gas in Astrakhan, for opening oil and gas reserves in the Barents Sea, for the joint production of methanol, and for coal liquification at Krasnojarsk in south-central Siberia (that is, the same general area in which the Eleventh Plan also calls for using inexpensive open pit coal in new thermal power stations at Kansk-Achinsk and at Ekibastuz). The USSR is also interested in cooperation in the construction of other coal-powered electricity generating plants, while West German firms would like to use Soviet mining technologies in inclined seams of coal.[1] A French-Soviet agreement in effect since 1975 provides a framework for French companies to undertake the building of a gas treatment complex and a plant for manufacturing

---

[1]*Nachrichten für Aussenhandel*, November 20, 1981.

compressors as well as for offshore exploration in the Barents Sea. In 1978, the United Kingdom and Romania concluded a contract for technical cooperation in the exploration and production of offshore oil and gas, including supply base construction as well as machinery and equipment.[1]

Japan's economic interest in energy prospects in eastern Siberia is also strong, notably in the South Yakutsk coal development project, the exploration and development of oil and gas in the Sakhalin Continental Shelf, and the exploration for natural gas at Yakutsk. All of these have for Japan the dual attraction of not only providing additional diversification in her access to sources of energy, but also creating new large demands for Japanese exports of machinery and equipment.

More recently, Japan has also felt the impact of the U.S. Government's embargo on the use of U.S. materials or technology in any energy projects in the Soviet Union. This action, taken as part of the Administration's package of sanctions against the Soviet Union for its role in Poland, will impede for a time the culmination of an oil and gas project off Sakhalin Island that has been underway since 1975. The result has been a cascade of protests from Japan, which appears to see itself losing much more than the Soviets as a consequence of the U.S. restrictions. The Soviet Government is apparently considering an abrogation of the joint contract for non-performance, and then assuming unilateral control of the project.

The United States, through two of its energy companies, was also interested at one time jointly with Japanese firms in the Yakutsk natural gas project, which contemplated a pipeline to an east coast port, bringing some 2 billion cubic feet of gas per day for liquification there, and then to be transported by LNG carriers in equal proportions to Japan and the United States. At various times U.S. firms have also been interested in supplying equipment for the Samotlor and Fedorovsk petroleum reserves in western Siberia, in providing offshore drilling platforms for use in the Caspian Sea, and in supplying equipment and technology for the exploration, development, and production of petroleum reserves offshore in the Arctic Ocean, as well as in the areas off Sakhalin Island that are also of interest to the Japanese. The Church Amendment to the U.S. Export-Import Bank Act in 1974, however, specifically forbids the Eximbank to make loans for energy development in the USSR. The recent actions of the U.S. Administration further impair prospects in the energy area with the USSR.

---

[1]A.F. Ewing, "Energy and East-West Cooperation," *Journal of World Trade Law*, Vol. XV, No. 3 (May/June 1981), pp. 226 ff.

Prospects mentioned are, to be sure, selective illustrations. A full list of prospective East-West business in the energy field would be much longer, and would include projects of potential interest to several other Trilateral countries. Moreover, there are also possibilities for joint research and development on alternative sources of energy, such as the collaboration of scientists at Princeton University with scientists from the USSR on processes for the production of energy through nuclear fusion. That work, of which there are several other counterparts such as that on magneto-hydrodynamics (on which Soviet scientists have in many respects advanced beyond the Americans), was initiated under the October 1972 U.S.-USSR agreements on scientific exchange. Those agreements included a specific treaty providing for work in nuclear fusion to continue through 1984. After Afghanistan that agreement ceased to have content, but was reactivated in December 1981, only to be interrupted again by the U.S. reaction to developments in Poland.

However, the aim of this study is not to list attractive trading possibilities for the businessmen of the Trilateral countries, nor to intrude into technical areas beyond the competence of the authors, but rather to outline principles affecting economic relations and to suggest an organizational framework for the kinds of trade or exchanges that may be appropriate. With respect to energy, the position reached by this study is that nations and firms should be free to develop any opportunities that are not forbidden by CoCom proscriptions, provided that they are consistent with the principle of diversification and are protected by adequate fall-back arrangements for any adverse contingency.

B. AGRICULTURE

Agricultural trade has come to play a crucial role in international politics as worldwide concern has increasingly focused on the problems and needs in the global distribution of food. The significance of such trade in East-West relations has become particularly prominent for several reasons. On the one hand, even while the CMEA countries have been trying to expand agricultural production, they have become increasingly dependent on agricultural imports. On the other hand, even though the United States has become increasingly dependent on agricultural exports to help its trade position and provide income for its farm sector, it has chosen to use sanctions on such exports as an instrument of its foreign policy, often without coordinating the sanctions with its allies. This has made agricultural trade the source of some conflict not only between East and West but also within the Western alliance. Potentially, however, there is much to be said for developing a regime of policies and agreements for stabilizing agricultural trade that could promote the long-term interests of both the CMEA members and the Trilateral countries.

Key Factors in the Development of Trade

During the two decades following World War II, the CMEA economies gave priority to investment goods (such as machinery and equipment) over consumption goods in their imports from the West. Indeed, the CMEA countries deliberately kept food imports low during those years and in that way maintained a modest surplus position in agricultural trade with the West.[1] The aim of their policies was, at the least, to sustain agricultural independence. However, by the late '50s, serious shortfalls in the Soviet agricultural sector led Khrushchev to initiate programs concentrating more effort on domestic agricultural development. Nonetheless, a crop failure in 1963 forced the Soviet Union to turn to the Western grain exporters in a major way (see Exhibit 8). The implication that Khrushchev's agricultural program had failed stirred a ferment of political dissatisfaction in Moscow and contributed to his dismissal. Still, a precedent for importing grain was established, and the succeeding leadership could more easily return to the Western markets when it again became necessary in 1966.

The most significant shift in the pattern of Soviet agricultural import policy came in the early '70s. In 1971 and 1972 Soviet production went from poor to worse. The Soviets took advantage of the recent initiatives establishing detente and purchased nearly 23 million metric tons of grain and soybeans on favorable terms in the crop year 1972/73. This was equivalent to about 15 percent of Soviet grain consumption as food and animal feed, and was more than twice the volume of the 1963/64 imports, the previous record. Since 1973, large imports of grain have been the rule rather than the exception for the Soviet Union (Exhibit 8).

The rapid increase of Soviet grain imports reflects a collision between production and consumption trends. On the production side, the Soviet Union has been unable to improve yields to the levels attained in the West. This is a function of both controllable and uncontrollable factors. Agricultural policies and management in the socialized sector tend to perpetuate inefficiency by limiting incentives to produce and market crops, by failing to coordinate effectively the application of

---

[1]CMEA agricultural exports consisted mainly of processed meats and beverages. Overall, agricultural goods represented 29 percent (or $633 million) of total CMEA exports in 1961, declining to 18 percent of exports (or $1,208 million) in 1971 as industrial exports grew. OECD, *Statistics of Foreign Trade, Series C.*

Exhibit 8

U.S.S.R. GRAIN PRODUCTION, TRADE, AND CONSUMPTION
1960-1981
(million metric tons)

Crop Year	Production	Trade			Principal Uses[a]	
		Imports	Exports	Net	Food	Feed
1960/61	125.5	0.8	7.0	+ 6.2	42	41
1961/62	130.8	0.8	8.4	+ 7.6	44	45
1962/63	140.2	0.6	8.3	+ 7.7	48	43
1963/64	107.5	10.4	4.7	− 5.7	47	32
1964/65	152.1	2.6	4.3	+ 1.7	45	44
1965/66	121.1	9.0	5.3	− 3.7	44	56
1966/67	171.2	3.9	5.3	+ 1.4	44	60
1967/68	147.9	2.3	6.4	+ 4.1	44	64
1968/69	169.5	1.2	7.4	+ 6.2	44	72
1969/70	162.4	1.8	7.6	+ 5.8	45	83
1970/71	186.8	1.3	8.5	+ 7.2	45	92
1971/72	181.2	8.3	6.9	− 1.4	45	93
1972/73	168.2	22.8	1.8	− 21.0	45	98
1973/74	222.5	11.3	6.1	− 5.2	45	105
1974/75	195.7	5.7	5.3	− 0.4	45	107
1975/76	140.1	26.1	0.7	− 25.4	45	89
1976/77	223.8	11.0	3.3	− 7.7	45	112
1977/78	195.7	18.9	2.3	− 16.8	45	122
1978/79[b]	237.4	15.6	2.8	− 12.8	46	125
1979/80[b]	179.2	31.0	0.8	− 30.2	46	126
1980/81[c]	189.2	35.0	1.0	− 34.0	47	118

[a] Production and net imports exceed these utilization totals due to seed and industrial uses, wastage, and changes in inventory
[b] preliminary
[c] estimate

Source: U.S. Department of Agriculture, "Agricultural Situation: USSR" (Washington: 1981) Table 4.

fertilizers and the use of machinery, and by allowing significant losses in transportation and storage. As a result, the Soviets must depend upon private plots for substantial amounts of produce, dairy products, and livestock. Meanwhile, despite the direction of a significant proportion of investment into state agriculture, Soviet productivity is still quite low.[1] To be sure, many of the Soviet Union's problems are less controllable. Land, water, and seasonal temperatures are not as favorable as in North America. With irregular weather patterns, Soviet agricultural production is inherently more volatile. Furthermore, the same factors have made it infeasible for large scale Soviet production of maize (corn), which is the basis of the highest acreage yields in the United States. Yet, despite these obstacles, the percentage rate of growth of Soviet grain production from 1960 to 1980 almost matched that of the United States, reflecting both improvement in yields and expansion of planted acreage.[2] Even so, the volume of production has fallen short of declared goals.

On the consumption side, the demand for grain has expanded much more rapidly in the Soviet Union than in the West, primarily because of the shift in meat production policy initiated by Khrushchev and extended by Brezhnev and Kosygin. The expansion of meat production depends heavily on increased feed grain consumption, and indeed, 75 percent of the increase in Soviet grain consumption from 1960 to 1980 represents increased feed grain consumption (Exhibit 8). Nearly all of the Soviet Union's demand for grain imports (apart from that caused by poor harvests) can be attributed to policies which have sought to increase the availability of meat to the Soviet consumer.

Grain production in Eastern Europe has historically been more stable than in the Soviet Union. Nevertheless, the region has consistently been a grain importer. The Soviets provided East Europe with most of its grain imports in the '50s and '60s, but the East Europeans were forced to turn to the West in the '70s as the Soviet Union shifted from being a net grain exporter to a net importer. Soviet grain exports to Eastern Europe declined from an average of about 7 million metric tons annually in the '60s, to about 4 million metric tons in the '70s, to virtually nothing in 1980.

Meanwhile, East European grain demand has been growing faster than domestic production, for precisely the same reason that Soviet

---

[1]See Karl-Eugen Wadekin, "Soviet Agriculture's Dependence on the West,"*Foreign Affairs*, Spring 1982: "The Soviet agricultural work force was tantamount to 5.6 workers per 100 acres of arable and perennial crop land, about as many as on the small farms of Western Europe, and about ten times more (in full-time equivalents) than in the United States." (p.896)

[2]The Soviet rate of increase is, of course, measured from a lower initial base. Average yields for wheat production, the Soviet Union's major crop, are still only about 70 percent of U.S. yields.

demand has grown, that is, they have responded to consumer desires for an increased availability of meat. Reflecting this, per capita meat consumption in Eastern Europe has increased by 50 percent since 1971.[1] Feed grain accounts for virtually all the growth of East European grain imports.

Until 1980, when the Afghanistan sanctions were imposed, the United States was the principal supplier of grains and soybeans to the CMEA countries. At the same time, the CMEA countries had become an important market for U.S. agricultural exports. In 1979, the value of such exports to the CMEA was $4.26 billion, two-thirds of which went to the Soviet Union. These exports represented approximately 23 percent of total U.S. grain and soybean exports. Conversely, U.S. exports in 1979 represented over half of total East European grain and soybean imports, and nearly 70 percent of total Soviet grain and soybean imports.

But with the imposition of sanctions against the Soviet Union in 1980, the value of U.S. agricultural exports to the Soviet Union was reduced from 1979 by nearly 60 percent, at a time when Soviet import requirements were increasing.[2] Compared with expected shipments during 1980, the embargo represented a reduction of from 13 to 16 percent of worldwide U.S. grain exports.[3] U.S. exports to Eastern Europe, however, continued to grow from 1979 to 1980, substantially replacing reduced Soviet shipments of grains to its CMEA partners. This, as previously mentioned, represented a loophole in the sanctions through which the Soviets offset about 1.5 million metric tons of their own grain import needs.

By comparison with the trade in grains, Trilateral-CMEA trade in other agricultural commodities has been moderate and fairly balanced.[4] Excluding grains and soybeans, the bulk of the agricultural trade of the CMEA countries is with Western Europe. Such trade accounted for about $1.50 billion in turnover in 1980, or only about 6 percent of total trade between Western Europe and the CMEA

---

[1]By comparison, Soviet per capita meat consumption has increased only about 12 percent in the same period, to 56 kilograms per capita in 1980. Indeed, meat production has been stagnant since 1975. (USDA, "Agricultural Situation: USSR," April 1981, pp. 6, 34, 36.) East European consumption in 1979 and 1980 ranged from 62 kilograms for Bulgaria and Romania to around 71 kilograms for Hungary and Poland to over 85 kilograms for Czechoslovakia and East Germany. (USDA, "Agricultural Situation: Eastern Europe," May 1981, p. 36.)

[2]Grains and soybeans constitute virtually all U.S. agricultural exports to the USSR.

[3]Data supplied to the authors orally by the Foreign Agricultural Service of the U.S. Department of Agriculture. This did not result in an equal net reduction of total exports, however, since some of the grain eventually went to other export markets.

[4]For the Soviet Union, the major exception is sugar, which the Soviets import at premium prices and in massive quantities from Cuba as a mechanism for providing support for the Cuban economy.

countries.[1] This sector of trade has been quite static during a period of otherwise dramatic growth in East-West trade.[2]

Comparative Vulnerability to Sanctions

The combination of interrelations in agricultural trade between East and West has become a source of vulnerability for both sides. The Soviet response to recent crop failures demonstrates that they are no longer willing to liquidate livestock herds to reduce grain consumption, out of concern over the domestic reduction in meat supplies. Indeed, having embarked on the path of higher consumption, the Soviets are eager to close the gap between domestic per capita meat supplies and the greater consumption in Eastern Europe. The more meat becomes a benchmark of the quality of life in the CMEA countries, the more feed grain and soybeans they will need, and the more they will depend upon Western imports for the foreseeable future.

On the other hand, Western grain producers are significantly dependent on the CMEA market for their own incomes. Despite the partial redistribution of markets after the Afghanistan embargo and the extensive government countermeasures to compensate farmers,[3] the loss of Soviet orders appears to have kept grain prices lower than they otherwise would have been. This exacerbated the drop in farm net income in the U.S. from $33 billion in 1979 to $20 billion in 1980. Nor was this the only manifestation of the economic loss to the United States, since related sectors, including shipping, fertilizers, and farm equipment manufacturing, were also hurt by the reduction of exports and incomes. To some extent, however, this loss was counterbalanced by the moderation of domestic food prices.

The U.S. partial embargo of agricultural exports to the Soviet Union was considered a failure, in part, because it inflicted very little cost on the Soviets; because it had no apparent effect on Soviet action in Afghanistan; and because the sensitivity of the U.S. political system to the farming sector caused the embargo to be lifted abruptly in April 1981 without consulting any allies.[4] The principal reason why the

[1]OECD, *Statistics of Foreign Trade, Series A.* Data for EEC.

[2]If forest products are included in the definition of "agriculture," there has been some increase in such trade, primarily in the form of CMEA exports to Trilateral countries. The largest component in value terms has been the export of timber and timber products by the Soviet Union to Japan.

[3]For a discussion of these countermeasures see "Report by the Comptroller General of the United States: Lessons to be Learned from Offsetting the Impact of the Soviet Grain Sales Suspension" (Washington: U.S. General Accounting Office, July 1981).

[4]Despite attempts to compensate farmers fully for any losses suffered because of the embargo, the farming community backlash against the embargo was tremendous. Mr. Reagan incorporated opposition to the agricultural embargo into his platform in his presidential campaign; and in 1981, Congress enacted legislation aimed at preventing the selective use of agriculture as an economic sanction. Supporters of the measure point out that had the legislation been in effect in January 1980, the Treasury would have been required to pay farmers over $25 billion to compensate for the embargo.

USSR was so impervious to the embargo, however, was the inability of the United States to persuade other exporters to cooperate on a widespread and continuing scale. That enabled the Soviets to meet almost all their grain import needs elsewhere, most notably through Argentina. While Canada did limit its exports of grain to previous "traditional" levels during the 1979/80 crop year, her grain exports were expanded rapidly at the beginning of the 1980/81 year. The Common Market meanwhile nearly doubled its grain sales to the USSR in 1980 over the previous year. The Soviets were also able to manage their import requirements by controlling feed consumption and reducing shipments to Eastern Europe.[1]

At the same time, the Soviets also replaced a part of the fertilizer shipments suspended by the United States. The Soviets had signed a twenty-year agreement with Occidental Petroleum providing for U.S. exports of phosphates to the USSR in exchange for Soviet deliveries of ammonia, potash, and urea. When the United States suspended the phosphate shipments early in 1980 as a means of reinforcing the grain embargo, the return flow of Soviet ammonia nevertheless continued, though restricted by a new U.S. import ceiling of one million metric tons annually. The Soviets, meanwhile, in great need of phosphates particularly suited for improving their own kinds of soil, replaced part of the embargoed U.S. supply with less satisfactory grades from Morocco and Mexico and some higher grades from a Belgian company. This U.S. suspension, however, was also lifted early in 1981.[2]

Thus, despite the high degree of Soviet dependence on imported grain and other agricultural products, it has been able to limit its dependence on the United States, shifting her from prime supplier to supplier of last resort. Nevertheless, since the United States presently controls over 50 percent of the world's exportable grain and soybean production, and since Soviet production is not likely to catch up with consumption in the near future, it will be difficult for the Soviet Union to escape some dependence on U.S. agriculture. Still, the inability of the United States to develop a coordinated policy with other exporters, and the lack of political will domestically to continue the U.S. embargo alone, suggest that a U.S.-led agricultural embargo would not be a credible threat under currently prevailing conditions.

---

[1] Although some argue that the embargo imposed a significant cost on the Soviets because of the premium they had to pay for grain elsewhere, and because there was a certain inconvenience factor, it is not clear that the premium was much greater than the cost of U.S. grain would have been, had prices not been somewhat depressed by the overhang of the embargoed U.S. supply.

[2] This study's conclusion that the Afghanistan sanctions were ineffectual is not intended to imply that nothing should have been done to demonstrate deep concern over the Soviet invasion. The question of sanctions is discussed more fully in Section III, beginning on p. 83.

In 1979, of all the sectors of East-West trade, U.S. agricultural sales to Soviet and East European markets constituted the most significant example of export dependence.[1] Concurrently, the Soviet dependence on the United States for grain was the most significant Eastern exposure to a single Western supplier. Yet the ability of the Soviets to cope with the grain embargo — while the United States had less success in finding alternative markets and withstanding domestic political pressure — demonstrated some of the limitations on any future use of the "grain weapon" by the United States.

Proposals
The mutual vulnerability of Eastern importers and Western exporters can also be seen as the basis of mutual self-interest. Though the specific goals of each country may be distinct, the elements of key regional interests can be broadly outlined.

For the West, the key economic consideration is maintaining the stability of the commodities markets, which will, in turn, help stabilize farm income and food prices. At the same time, the Western nations want to ensure that export prices reflect the full economic value of their exports, lest they inadvertently end up making implicit transfer payments to their CMEA customers.

The focus of Western interests is to avoid a recurrence of the very disruptive impact that Soviet purchases had on the world markets in 1972/73. When the Soviet Union came shopping for grain in 1972, the U.S. Department of Agriculture saw an opportunity to unload the burdensome surplus stocks the United States had accumulated, and so it did not stand in the way as the Soviets obtained 19 million metric tons of wheat, maize, and soybeans from American stocks and production in 1972/73. Since the United States carries such a large proportion of the world's grain stocks,[2] the depletion of U.S. stocks created a critical if temporary world shortage and sent grain and soybean prices shooting up 200 to 300 percent in 1973, generating turmoil and hostility domestically and internationally among the market economies and beyond. Despite large Soviet purchases, Japan was (and is) still the largest importer of U.S. grains and soybeans. Serious friction resulted when

---

[1]Again, exports to the CMEA represented 23 percent of U.S. grain and soybean exports in 1979. By comparison, West Germany's sales of iron and steel products to the CMEA countries represented about 20 percent of total exports of these products in the 1974-79 period, and these shipments were less than one-quarter of the value of the U.S. grain. Currently, with the embargo lifted, U.S. grain shipments to the CMEA countries are estimated to be 15 to 20 percent of total grain exports for 1981/82.
[2]USDA, "The 1981/82 World Grain Outlook," December 11, 1981, p. 2.

domestic pressure led the U.S. Government to briefly bar soybean exports to Japan in 1973. Avoiding a similar episode in the future should understandably be high on the list of Western priorities.

The interests of the CMEA countries are consistent with Western interests, though different in focus. On the one hand, the CMEA countries wish to maintain open access to Western food supplies. On the other hand, they are eager to increase the productivity of their own agricultural sectors. The goal of the international and domestic agricultural policies of the CMEA countries is to maintain constant, if gradual, increases in the domestic standard of living by providing improved food supplies at stable prices. Success in the pursuit of this goal is critical, since each regime perceives that its domestic support is importantly affected by the extent to which it achieves such objectives.

The growing interdependence of Eastern and Western interests embodies the paradox of Western policies toward the East. Apparently, but ironically, the United States (and to some extent Canada) depends on CMEA markets for disposal of a sizable part of its agricultural exports. But agricultural sales to the CMEA countries are not of particular importance for other Trilateral regions, which look to the CMEA markets for other kinds of trade. Such differences can inherently lead to the kinds of friction within the Trilateral group that have flared up again in 1982, as the United States attempted to block the European-Soviet gas pipeline arrangements while continuing to sell a maximum amount of U.S. grain to the Soviet Union. It is consequently important, as suggested further below, to find ways of satisfying the mutual interest of the East and West in agricultural relations without compromising the political or strategic goals of either.

Export Pricing
To avoid exporting food at prices below economic cost, the Western nations should work toward phasing out some production subsidies and recapturing others. Throughout the West, key sectors of agriculture are heavily subsidized. This raises concern over whether agricultural resources are being used as efficiently as possible. These subsidies are the product of social and political, as well as economic, goals. In Europe, the Common Agricultural Policy (CAP) within the EEC provides substantial pricing premiums to producers of such products as grain, milk, and sugar, and governments then have to subsidize the export of the surpluses that result from the stimulation of the artificially high domestic prices. Similarly, in Japan, huge subsidies for rice production are the result of both a national commitment to self-

sufficiency in rice and the political power of the Japanese farmers. Although the subsidies in both Europe and Japan may not be economically optimal, they clearly have strong political support.

In the United States, support programs for grains and soybeans are now structured more as insurance and short-term financing schemes than as income guarantees. Farmers generally sell their crops at market-determined prices. Still, the government provides substantial indirect subsidies in the form of water resources, concessional credit, and tax incentives. Recent declines in prices, however, have brought them down into the range where direct price supports come back into operation. In addition, the previously discarded "set-aside" subsidy program, in which the government pays farmers to limit their planted acreage, is re-emerging as a means of limiting the collapse of farm income. Thus the market-determined prices do not necessarily reflect the true economic value of the crops even in the United States.

Aided by such policies, as well as by benevolent climatic and soil conditions, the United States and Canada have generated large exportable supplies of grain. Moreover, subsidies and the artificially high domestic prices stimulate production, but they also depress consumption in Western Europe and Japan. Consequently, Western Europe has recently become a significant net exporter of grain at reduced prices. Even so, in most years since 1960, the developing countries as a group have not been able to absorb the overhanging surpluses. Thus, strong pressures have built up to market these surpluses to the large and comparatively wealthy CMEA countries, with their growing demand for feed grain. To the extent that export prices to the CMEA countries are kept artificially low by policies that directly and indirectly offset the subsidized domestic food prices of the West, the Western exporting countries are in fact losing money with every bushel of maize or other crops that they sell to the Soviet Union and the countries of Eastern Europe.

At the risk of offering a counsel of perfection, this study suggests that wherever subsidies and price supports act as substitutes for more direct income supports, they should be phased out and replaced (if subsidies of some form are a political necessity) with policies that create less distortion in the world commodity markets. In the EEC, for example, the support of low-income rural areas through holding domestic prices at high levels results in windfall profits to wealthy farmers while providing minimally adequate incomes to the marginal farmers. The same prices act as a regressive tax on consumers. It would clearly seem preferable that such farm support should be provided through general tax and transfer payments systems, to the extent possible, in order to bring domestic prices more nearly in line with world price levels. On the other hand, where subsidies are provided indirectly, such as through concessional credit or subsidized fertilizer or seed or water, the low prices and costs of the resulting products could be approximately offset by collecting an excise tax.

With respect to credit terms, the Western exporting countries should in any event continue to work toward reducing the direct subsidies provided through artificially low interest charges in export financing arrangements. Whether any such policies aimed at bringing the terms of Trilateral exports to the CMEA countries into line with real economic costs can be politically palatable is, of course, still an open question. The desirability of achieving a political consensus on a reasonable uniformity in approach is nonetheless compelling, both because of the meaningful impact on the terms of trade and because the hostility engendered in the past by conflicts among various aspects of the agricultural policies of the Trilateral nations has been a disturbing cause of fragmentation within the Western alliance.

Improving Productivity in the CMEA Countries
A logical alternative to the expanding of CMEA demand on the world markets lies in increasing the productivity of the agricultural sectors of the CMEA countries themselves. Because of the strong influence of social and political factors in Soviet and East European agriculture, the ability of the West to assist in improving productivity is severely limited. Potentially, however, the CMEA countries could benefit greatly from obtaining (on a commercial basis) increased access to Western skills and equipment in all aspects of agriculture — from production and storage to transportation and processing.

To what extent, however, would increased production in the East affect the West? All other things being equal, the better the Soviet crop, the lower the exports to the CMEA countries from the West, and the greater the pressure to dispose of crop surpluses elsewhere at lower prices. While the scenario is attractive for grain importers and consumers, particularly for the undernourished, grain-importing developing countries, it represents a trade-off for the grain exporters of the West, where farm income would be hurt. Ironically, the EEC, locked into the Common Agricultural Policy, would fare worse if increased agricultural production in the CMEA countries were followed by a lowering of agricultural prices around the world. Though EEC farmers would not be hurt, EEC consumers would not benefit, and EEC treasuries would certainly have to spend even more than at present to subsidize their exports.

However, in a world confronting grain deficiencies for a growing population, the net gain from a growth of production in any potentially productive area must be considered a positive contribution. Indeed it would appear useful, quite apart from whatever may be done *vis-à-vis* the USSR itself, to focus on commercial projects that enhance East European agricultural production. Increases there would reduce the dependence of some of these countries on the Soviet Union for food and agricultural supplies.[1] Since this dependence is generally a burden on the USSR, the Soviets might welcome such a development. At the same time, improvements in production would ease one source of pressure on Eastern European hard currency reserves, which are now literally consumed by agricultural imports.

The Soviets have recently again been sharply increasing investment in their agricultural sector. In the 1976-80 Five-Year Plan, 27 percent of all new investment was targeted for agriculture, and in the 1981-85 Plan, a similar commitment has been made.[2] Nevertheless, the continued emphasis on an increased availability of meat makes it unlikely that the Soviet Union will be able to reduce materially its dependence upon Western maize and soybean imports in the near future, even if its wheat crop should improve greatly. Moreover, if world demand for all of the feed grains grows faster than the past pace of increases in production, any improvement of CMEA agricultural productivity should in the long term be in the interest of the West as well as the East.

And there is no question that the Soviet market for sales of virtually every form of Western agricultural equipment and services would be substantial for many years ahead. The keys to unlocking this potential are the needed agreement of Western governments to permit the exports, and the needed earnings by the USSR from other exports of its own, in order to pay for the imports. To a much lesser degree, the same opportunities and conditions would apply to Western exports of agricultural machinery and techniques to the other CMEA countries.

Market Stability and CMEA Access
While the commodities markets are among the closest approximations to the theoretical image of the competitive free market, there is a persuasive reason why the West might want to control access to the grain markets by the Soviet Union and its CMEA partners. That is because even in these markets, a large purchaser can have a substan-

---

[1]Although Hungary, Romania, and Bulgaria are net agricultural exporters overall, only Hungary is self-sufficient in grains.
[2]German Institute for Economic Research, "The CMEA Countries' Problematic Plan Targets," *op. cit.*

tially disruptive impact if the buying occurs abruptly and at times in massive volume. Such control can in theory be based on the purely economic desirability of regulating the access of an oligopsonistic buyer. But the case was more than theoretical in 1972, for example, after what was dubbed the "Great Grain Robbery." Since then, the mechanisms that have been developed for monitoring Soviet purchases, and for keeping the markets informed of potential Soviet demand, appear to be reasonably effective. To moderate the impact of swings in Soviet grain production on their own markets, and to increase their market share, Argentina, Brazil, and Canada have each negotiated a bilateral long-term sales agreement with the Soviet Union.[1] The United States meanwhile, however, has blocked re-negotiation of its long-term agreement as part of its response to the imposition of martial law in Poland.

In addition to these agreements concerning minimum availabilities of grain to the USSR, there is also a case to be made for convincing the Soviets to carry larger stocks, provided there could be substantial improvements in their grain storage systems. The Soviet Union has already shown some willingness to make such stockpiling arrangements in exchange for assured access to the grain markets under clearly established conditions. Meanwhile, it would clearly seem desirable for the Western nations to resume discussions among themselves aimed at improving the coordination of policies during periods of both shortage and surplus. The overall aim should be to come somewhat closer to a balancing among the Trilateral domestic requirements, the needs of developing countries, and indicated CMEA requirements. Fortunately, the markets themselves, through the expansion of the futures markets, as well as through the enlargement of facilities spurred by the growth in world grain trade, have increased their resistance to shocks.

None of this precludes the possibility that some Soviet provocation might again justify the imposition of a partial or total embargo of grain shipments to the Eastern countries. But a fuller knowledge of stocks, current availabilities, and prospective yields should restrain precipitate action by any one supplier in imposing an agricultural embargo. Recent experience has demonstrated that no single supplier, not even the United States, can effectively influence Soviet behavior by acting largely alone. From a more constructive perspective, however, there is no doubt that a return to the regularizing of relations between the

---

[1]These agreements will provide about one-quarter of the Soviet Union's expected import needs over the next five years. The contract with Argentina, for example, commits the Soviets to buy 4.5 million metric tons of grain a year, but they actually contracted for much more than that in 1981.

largest exporter (the United States) and the largest importer (the USSR) would contribute importantly toward a needed stability in the most elemental of the world's commodity markets.

C. TECHNOLOGY:
MACHINERY, MANUFACTURES, AND MINING

Energy and agriculture have only recently become key issues in East-West relations, reflecting the development of new patterns of world trade over the last decade. East-West technological trade, on the other hand, has been a subject of contention from the very beginning of the Cold War. More so than any other sector, technology has defined the gap between the economies of the CMEA and the Trilateral nations. Perhaps more importantly, since World War II technology has been at the core of the strategic competition between the two superpowers — from atom bombs to H-bombs, from sputniks to MIRVs, and from cruise missiles to "killer satellites."

Nonetheless, the technological gap between East and West creates a powerful pressure to trade. Much of the spectacular growth of the OECD nations since World War II has been founded on technology-based improvements in productivity. The CMEA nations, however, have been much less successful in developing and implementing new technologies in the civilian sectors of their economies. Over time, they have become increasingly willing and eager to import such technology from the West, and Western firms have generally been eager to supply products, licenses, plants, and equipment. But several factors have constrained such trade, including Western policies restricting the export of strategically important technology. Overall, however, a tremendous range of opportunities is available outside the military sector for the West to exploit its trading advantage in technology — in manufacturing, machinery, transportation, and natural resource development.

The more binding constraint is the severe shortage of hard currency in the East to pay for the imports of technology. But if the Eastern regimes are to fulfill their promises of economic progress, they will have to use their hard currency more efficiently to increase such imports, and they will have to apply that technology more productively throughout their economies. In the Soviet Union in particular, the creative results of superior scientific achievements often get lost on the way to engineering implementation, with the exception, of course, of military technology, which always has a commanding priority.

Significance of Trade in Technology

It is difficult to quantify technology trade very precisely because of the various forms in which technology is embodied. Technology can simply refer to "know-how," which may be incorporated in a plant design or product design — commercially exported in the form of a license — or which may be transmitted through personnel training. Know-how is also transferred non-commercially through scientific exchanges, published literature, and industrial espionage. An even more subtle, but nonetheless critical, form of technology is embodied in management techniques — including methods of decision-making, monitoring, and control. Technology can also be transmitted more concretely as a product, such as a sophisticated oil-drilling bit, machine tool, or computer. But some products less commonly included in East-West technology trade, such as high quality steel and pipeline, should also be included in the consideration of technology issues insofar as they substitute for technology not available in the CMEA countries. The most comprehensive form of technology transfer, however, is the export of turnkey plants, which includes both know-how and products.

In these various forms, technology has been a dominant component of CMEA imports from the OECD nations. If machinery and transportation equipment alone are taken as a proxy, technology has represented 30 to 40 percent of CMEA imports from the OECD since 1961 (see Exhibit 1). For the Soviet Union, this percentage has been even higher. And if the technology embodied in certain manufactures and in specialty steel products were included, the percentage would be higher still. As Zaleski and Wienert point out in their overview of East-West technology trade, the technological component of CMEA imports is far higher than for world trade in general, or even for trade among the advanced industrialized countries.[1] According to one Soviet analyst, about 80 percent of the cooperation agreements between the CMEA countries and the West incorporate provisions for technology transfer.[2]

This pattern in CMEA imports reflects both policy decisions and structural factors. Structurally, the relative abundance of raw materials within the Soviet Union leads to a natural preference for technology-based imports. As a matter of policy, CMEA imports were initially constrained both by Stalinist prescriptions aiming for autarky and by

---

[1]Eugene Zaleski and Helgard Wienert, *Technology Transfer Between East and West* (Paris: OECD, 1980), pp. 67-91.

[2]V. Malkevich, *East-West Economic Cooperation and Technological Exchange* (Moscow: USSR Academy of Sciences, 1981), p.105. This text, with a foreword by Professor Georgi Skorov, is particularly interesting as it provides an up-to-date Soviet perspective on the history of and prospects for trade in technology.

Western policies seeking to isolate the Soviet economy. Aware of the dangerous limitations of Stalin's approach, Khrushchev undertook to gain access to Western technology within the new environment of "peaceful coexistence." At the 22nd Party Congress in 1961, Khrushchev was quite emphatic about the importance of technology, including foreign technology:

> It is essential that we make use of everything that science and technology give us in our country more rapidly and exhaustively, and take more boldly all the best that foreign experience can give.... In building communism, we cannot tolerate technological conservatism. You can't jump high fences on an old nag, as they say.[1]

The initial focus of Khrushchev's pursuit of Western technology was the importation of modern chemical plants, including in particular fertilizer technology for Soviet agricultural development. Indeed, Hanson estimates that through 1977, from 25 to 36 percent of Soviet technology imports each year were directed toward this "chemicalization" program.[2]

This reflects the sector specialization of CMEA technology import programs. Although overall technological imports have been a relatively small percent of annual Soviet investment in machinery and equipment, reaching a maximum estimated at 6 percent in the mid-'70s,[3] they have nevertheless had an important impact on certain sectors of the economy — chemical production being the most notable example. Other sectors of the Soviet economy in which imported technology has played a key role include transportation, computers, machine tools, shipping, and steel.[4]

Khrushchev's program to import Western technology was extended even further by Brezhnev and Kosygin. Probably the most significant turning point in East-West technological trade was the agreement between the Soviet Union and Italy's Fiat in 1966 to build a major automotive complex at Togliatti in the USSR. The significance of the Fiat agreement was not only in the scale of the project, but also in the unprecedented degree of interaction between the Soviets and Westerners, including the training of hundreds of Soviet technicians at Fiat's facilities in Italy.

---

[1]Quoted in Philip Hanson, *Trade and Technology in Soviet-Western Relations* (New York: Columbia University Press, 1981), p.93.
[2]*Ibid.*, p.138.
[3]*Ibid.*, pp.128-31.
[4]Zaleski and Wienert, *op.cit.*, pp.208-209.

The project framework has been a popular approach to importing technology, and a wave of projects was undertaken throughout the CMEA countries as detente brought greater flexibility to both East and West. The Kama River trucking complex in the Soviet Union involved importing over a billion dollars in equipment, plus long-term contracts for Western supplies and spare parts. Elsewhere in Eastern Europe similar projects have been negotiated: the Ursus complex in Poland and the Raba complex in Hungary produce farm machinery and related equipment, and in Romania a computer plant has been built with the assistance of the Digital Equipment Corporation (U.S.). Meanwhile, Japan negotiated several projects located in the far eastern Soviet Union, involving natural resource and infrastructure development, which required equipment with only a fairly basic level of technology. Other projects within the CMEA have included pharmaceutical plants, mining equipment and mine development, food processing, and, of course, oil and gas.

The logic of the project approach is that it provides the most complete transfer of technological know-how, materials, and production capability. Ultimately, this might seem to reduce CMEA dependence on Western technology, but as the Soviets have discovered at Kama River, ongoing relations with Western partners are necessary. Thus the effect is more likely an increase of dependence on Western firms. Recognizing this, some of the East European nations, particularly Romania and Hungary, are experimenting with various forms of "industrial cooperation" agreements which involve Western firms much more closely in the operation and management of imported facilities.

The impact of the transfer of Western technology to the Soviet Union and Eastern Europe is quite difficult to assess. Several studies of this have been attempted, and the conclusion seems to be that while the impact is certainly not negligible, it is also not particularly great. Reviewing the various analyses and emphasizing the difficulties of making such an assessment, Hanson concludes that productivity improvements from Western technology have possibly provided the Soviet Union with an incremental 0.5 percent of growth annually, at the most.[1] As mentioned, however, this contribution is concentrated in a few specific sectors. Another measure of the impact of the Soviet Union's program to improve its level of technology is the gap between

---

[1]Hanson, op.cit., pp. 144-155. Fewer studies have been attempted for Eastern Europe, with the result that judgments concerning the impact of technology imports in those countries more frequently rest on anecdotal evidence. In the case of Poland, which has been by far the largest East European importer of Western technology, large purchases of technical machinery or equipment that could not be efficiently utilized have most likely been a net drain on the resources and growth of the economy.

the technological capabilities of industry in the East and West. While again this varies substantially from sector to sector, the somewhat startling conclusion of most studies is that over the past fifteen to twenty years, the Soviet Union has not succeeded in significantly reducing its technological lag behind the West, except in limited special projects which can be saturated with very skilled manpower and advanced equipment and materials.[1]

Implications

There are several reasons for this persistent lag, not the least of which is that the Soviet Union has been shooting at a rapidly moving target. Despite significant improvements in Soviet industrial technology, Western technology has been progressing at least as fast. But there are also several reasons to believe that fundamental systemic weaknesses, creating problems in Soviet research, development, and implementation programs, may perpetuate the overall technological gap. Despite recent attempts to reform their R&D systems, development of new products and processes is still frequently separated from the enterprises that would use them by several bureaucratic intermediaries.

Furthermore, once new technology, whether imported or indigenous, is implemented, the Soviet record for diffusing that technology to other enterprises and other sectors is quite spotty. Even in key sectors of high technology, such as computers, where one might expect heavy emphasis on diffusion, investigation has suggested that very little circulation of the technology has taken place.[2] On the other hand, it does appear that chemical plant technology has been extended within the Soviet Union, and the imported technology of the Togliatti auto facility has been applied to tractor plants and even steelworks. Still, even analysts within the Soviet Union have expressed concern that not only are examples of such diffusion limited, but Soviet industry has also failed to update imported technology once it is in place. Although techniques such as "reverse engineering" — a method of recreating the production process for a high technology item — accelerate the rate of absorption of foreign technology, development of these techniques does little to advance indigenous innovation. These problems in innovation and diffusion reflect bottlenecks in information flow and the lack of incentives at both the individual and the enterprise level.

---

[1]The best known and broadest of these studies is R. Amann, J. M. Cooper, and R. W. Davies, eds., *The Technological Level of Soviet Industry* (New Haven: Yale University Press, 1977).

[2]Ron Scheiderman, "High Technology Flow," *Electronica*, January 8, 1976, quoted in Zaleski and Wienert, *op. cit.*, pp. 208-209.

Another problem in Soviet and East European technological progress is the difficulty Eastern enterprises have had achieving levels of productivity equivalent to those attained in the West with the same technology. This also appears to be a function of systemic weaknesses, including internal management problems, such as a tendency to overman, and external supply problems, which, for example, have forced many chemical plants to operate well below capacity. Supply problems have increased the attractiveness of industrial cooperation agreements that include Western sources of supply for certain critical items. Hard currency constraints, however, have limited the willingness of CMEA governments to approve such arrangements in recent years.

The continuing technological gap between the CMEA countries and the West represents a substantial opportunity for Western firms. The CMEA area represents a vast and comparatively wealthy market for Western exports of licenses, products, and plants. Nonetheless, there are several problems with expanding technological trade with the CMEA economies. From a political perspective, the key concern is the contribution of Western technology to Soviet military capability. The studies referred to above, however, suggest that Western exports of civilian technology have not had a relevant impact on Soviet military technology. Further, since CMEA nations only import proven commercial technology, such technology is likely to be several years behind the state of the art. There have been difficulties on the Western side, however, as firms have found that the export control mechanisms of their own countries are in some cases so cumbersome that they frequently act as a disincentive to export. Clearly, these mechanisms can be improved (as discussed further in outlining suggested changes in CoCom in Section III). But even beyond such obstacles, the problems remain that many Western firms have encountered in the process of negotiating with the ministries responsible for many of the state-run enterprises — problems often described as excruciatingly frustrating.

While imports of technology tend to create Eastern dependence on Western firms, there is also the danger that Western firms — indeed, entire sectors — may become dependent on CMEA markets. The most vivid recent example of this is the importance to certain firms in West Germany, France, the United Kingdom, Italy, and elsewhere, of providing materials for the Urengoi pipeline project. Western governments have in this instance carefully reviewed the degree to which their firms might have been unduly influenced by the desire to support employment and production levels, at the risk of becoming too dependent on the resulting flow of Soviet gas. To be sure, some of the Soviet statements designed to interest Western firms in the opportunities for trade would appear to suggest that they are attempting to exploit precisely such leverage.[1]

The most significant problem, however, is the constraint that pervades all East-West trade, namely the shortage of hard currency. This has prompted CMEA state-run enterprises to press for countertrade agreements calling for payment in goods rather than cash. In some cases, this may be reasonably attractive to the Western firm, especially in the case of resource development projects that provide Western firms with new sources of supply. In most cases in which countertrade involves manufactured goods, however, it has not been very successful. At times, Western firms are asked to take back goods and market them in regions that are either unprofitable or are areas to which the firm already provides competing products. There have been, however, some notable examples of CMEA success at exporting manufactured goods, such as the new Hungarian bus.

Concern for CMEA hard currency shortages, though, should not force Western governments to agree to concessional financing or under-pricing of exports as a means of maintaining employment and trade balances. While CoCom provides a forum for managing Western strategic vulnerability, a separate forum may be appropriate to coordinate Western export policies that relate to pricing, financing, and unfair trade practices. This is discussed in the section on Finance below, and is further developed in Section III in the suggestions on multilateral initiatives.

D. SERVICES AND OTHER NON-MERCHANDISE TRADE

Despite the dominance of merchandise in the trade of the East and West, there are other components of trade that have been of increasing importance to the CMEA countries, primarily the Soviet Union, as sources of hard currency earnings. Expanded trade in services — including shipping, insurance, and tourism — has been actively promoted by the CMEA countries. In addition, worldwide sales of gold and military equipment, also excluded from merchandise trade statistics, have become even more significant as producers of hard currency, although the market for Soviet military equipment is not, needless to say, to be found in the Trilateral regions.

As in the West, the service sectors in the socialist economies have been growing more rapidly than the industrial sectors. Nevertheless,

---

[1]See, for example, "A Kremlin 'Trade Manifesto' for the 1980s," *Journal of Commerce*, January 8, 1982, p. 1A.

these sectors are still generally smaller than in the market economies. This reflects the ideological conception that many services are non-productive, as well as the policy of CMEA governments to focus on the development of the industrial sector. Still, the Soviet Five-Year Plan for 1976-80, which called for increased investment in services, demonstrates a growing awareness of the legitimate role of services in the economy and in earning foreign exchange.[1] Conversely, sales of any of the service items from West to East have largely been embodied in various forms of technology transfer.

Shipping has become a substantial source of hard currency earnings for the USSR, with revenues of over one-half billion dollars in both 1977 and 1978.[2] The Soviets pointedly negotiate shipping arrangements along with their trade agreements, attempting to extract the most business on the best terms.[3] The Soviet Union has also aggressively promoted its own shipping in competition for non-Soviet trade throughout the world. Indeed, Western carriers have complained that the Soviets are practicing predatory pricing — charging rates below cost in an effort to drive other shipping lines out of business. In recent years, however, increased imports of grain, requiring some non-Soviet ships, have diminished net hard currency earnings from shipping.

The strategic implications of Soviet shipping practices worry some Western observers. By pricing shipping services at their marginal cost — or perhaps even lower — the USSR is able to maintain a very large merchant fleet, which would be available for military purposes if necessary. Thus some argue that the West, to the extent that it permits this practice, is crippling its own merchant fleet while effectively sustaining the Soviet fleet. As it is, however, international negotiations on fair-trading practices in the service sectors are still in their infancy. Early efforts to restrain Soviet shipping practices have had some results in rate adjustments on certain routes since 1980, but further mechanisms for dealing with such problems on a multilateral basis should be further encouraged.

---

[1] A more detailed discussion of the services sector of CMEA economies is included in Ronald Kent Shelp, *Beyond Industrialization: Ascendancy of the Global Service Economy* (New York: Praeger, 1981), pp. 41-59.

[2] Other transportation services, such as air and rail freight and passenger services, are insignificant by comparison. Paul G. Ericson and Ronald S. Miller, "Soviet Foreign Economic Behavior: A Balance of Payments Perspective," *Soviet Economy in a Time of Change*, Volume 2, Joint Economic Committee, U.S. Congress (Washington, D.C.: October 10, 1979), pp. 208-243.

[3] The U.S.-USSR Maritime Agreement, negotiated in the early '70s, called for U.S. and Soviet trade to be split evenly between ships of the two countries. President Reagan, however, allowed this Agreement to expire as part of his package of sanctions in response to the Polish crisis in December 1981. The extremely low level of U.S.-Soviet trade in non-grain items makes this a somewhat symbolic gesture. Grain shipments under the U.S.-Soviet grain sales agreement separately follow the provisions of the Maritime Agreement, but enforcement by the United States has apparently been quite irregular.

Similarly, the Soviet Union and other East European countries press their trading partners to obtain cargo insurance contracts from the CMEA state insurance companies, covering shipments of both imports and exports. This has been a source of some irritation to Western insurers. CMEA enterprises have also branched out into the other areas of insurance. Ingosstrakh, the Soviet state insurance agency, has expanded its offices overseas and is competing for non-Soviet business. Indeed, one subsidiary was for a time involved in reinsuring the U.S. Overseas Private Investment Corporation. In effect, the Soviets were insuring U.S. firms against expropriation in developing countries. Such expansion into non-CMEA markets is one of the rare examples of overseas investment by Soviet enterprises. Construction and engineering contracting is another example of CMEA enterprises operating outside the territory of the CMEA countries, as they now bid for contracts in several of the developing countries.

Another highly visible effort of the CMEA countries has been their promotion of tourism in their own countries. The East European countries have been especially energetic about enticing their West European neighbors to visit and bring hard currency. In addition to opening tourism offices in the West, the CMEA countries have attempted to spark interest through cultural exchanges and promotions. The Moscow Olympics were the centerpiece of the recent Soviet efforts to promote tourism. The post-Afghanistan Carter boycott, however, substantially reduced the hard currency revenues from the Olympics, and visits by Americans, a large component of Soviet tourism, were down 75 percent in 1980. Meanwhile, the Soviet Union has also been aggressively promoting passenger and ocean cruise services.

Sales of gold and military equipment are much more important than services as sources of hard currency, especially for the Soviet Union. Data on these sales, though, are scarce because the Soviet Union is particularly secretive about them. Yet, according to one estimate, even though less than half of Soviet military sales are for hard currency, this amounted to over $1.5 billion annually in the late '70s.[1] Some East European countries, such as the GDR and Czechoslovakia, also appear to earn some hard currency from their own sales of military equipment.

Gold sales by the Soviet Union appear to be larger still, though more volatile. This reflects the somewhat discretionary nature of these sales, which are executed according to Soviet hard currency needs. The value of these sales is estimated to have fluctuated in the $1 to $3 billion range

---

[1]Ericson and Miller, *op. cit.*, p. 214.

in the late '70s.[1] Recently, after relatively low volume in 1980, these sales appear to have accelerated dramatically as the Soviet Union experiences pressure on its hard currency reserves. Some analysts estimate that Soviet gold sales doubled in volume between 1980 and 1981, and continued to be heavy in 1982. Historically, the Soviets have timed their sales according to market conditions, but lately they have been forced to continue selling despite the gold market's weakness, which they have certainly exacerbated.[2] One approach the USSR has taken to reduce this impact has been to use gold as collateral for loans rather than selling it outright.[3]

The extent to which credit from the West has in the past, and may in the future, relieve pressures on Soviet and other East European hard currency reserves is the subject of the next subsection.

E. FINANCE

The Role and Volume of Western Credit to the East
Credit has played a critical role in the expansion plans of the CMEA countries. That is because they have centered their import strategy on financing the purchase of new technology from the West with credits, in the expectation that the resulting added production would in time provide exports to service the debt. While perhaps a quarter of total indebtedness has been rollover credits related to normal commercial trade, the larger proportion of the borrowings from the West has been for maturities beyond a year and related to longer-term investments in equipment that may not provide exportable products for several years.[4]

The bulk of the $66.3 billion net debt outstanding for all CMEA countries at the end of 1980 was in Euro-currency bank credits of various maturities; only Poland and Hungary have been borrowers in the international bond markets. Except for Hungary and East Germany, however, there were no sizable increases in borrowing from the West in 1981. While there are reports of loan commitments to the USSR by Austria for over one-half billion dollars in 1982, the flow of new credits from West to East has otherwise been limited to credits for Hungary arranged by the BIS to help offset withdrawals of deposits from Hungary that occurred as a repercussion of the Polish crisis.

---

[1]*Ibid.*
[2]"The Impact of Soviet Gold Sales," *The New York Times*, January 5, 1982, p. D1.
[3]Swiss banking sources estimate that the Soviets have recently been arranging up to $3.2 billion in loans in this manner. "Soviets Use Gold as Collateral to Back Loans," *The Wall Street Journal*, March 25, 1982, p.32.
[4]The volume and growth of CMEA debt to the West has already been outlined in Section I and in Exhibit 6.

In view of the generally weak nature of the CMEA economies in 1982, most of them will for some time scarcely be able to earn enough in net hard currency exports, after paying for minimal essential imports, to cover their debt service requirements; there will be little if any balance left over to pay for additional imports of capital goods. The hard implication is that, whatever else the East or the West may initiate in the future to revive the impetus for trade, very little increase in trade can actually occur unless Western credit of some form is available to prime the growth. The greater immediate risk, though, is that exports to the West may decline to the point where even existing debt cannot be serviced. Thus far the only actual problem areas are Poland and Romania, but they spread a fog of uncertainty over the credit standings of all the other countries of Eastern Europe.

The Problem of Credits to Poland

The case of Poland is the most complex and troublesome because internal economic disintegration led to a shutting down, and then only a partial reactivation, of most production — both for home consumption and for export. Apart from all of the distressing social and human implications and the wide-reaching political consequences of the continuing Polish crisis, the result on the financial side has been debilitating. Initially, the debt owed to Western governments in 1981 was rescheduled, partly as a gesture of political forbearance. As for the commercial bank debt, Poland has barely been able to meet the interest payments that were due in 1981, and she accomplished that only after a considerable delay into 1982. Once the interest was paid, the outstanding portion of debt still due the banks in 1981 was rescheduled.

Since early 1982 an almost continuous series of contacts with Western government credit institutions and commercial banks has been under way by Polish officials concerning the possible deferral of the installments of outstanding debt maturing in 1982. The overall Western debt still outstanding in 1982 totals about $27 billion, of which $11 billion is in state-guaranteed credits and $16 billion is commercial credits.[1] Thus far, because of the political situation in Poland, the Western governments have put off actual negotiations concerning their more than $6 billion of credits due in 1982. The Western commercial banks, however, have begun negotiations in mid-year with respect to their $4 billion of 1982 maturities, but they have insisted that provision must be made for meeting the interest payments due during the year before postponement of maturities can be definitively agreed upon.

---

[1] All data on 1982 debt are as of mid-year. "Western Bankers Plan Talks on Rescheduling Poland's $4 Billion Debt," *The Wall Street Journal*, July 2, 1982, p. 17.

In a way, Poland illustrates the classical credit dilemma: While the borrower is not strong enough to merit additional credit, the lenders have already committed so much that they cannot afford to let the borrower default. Indeed, despite petulant demands for a declaration of default coming from many in the West who would like to apply pressure on the Polish Government for what has happened, there has been steadfast resistance to such action by all responsible financial officials and bankers in the West. Default would gain nothing and lose much. It would relieve Poland of a sense of obligation to make current payments, of either interest or principal. Moreover, it would remove any role that Western creditors might otherwise have in consulting with Poland on the revitalizing of its economy, the restructuring of its plant, and the energizing of its population. For without further outside assistance from somewhere, it is doubtful that Poland can have much more than a rudimentary subsistence economy for a rather long time, with the alternative only of being pushed further into the condition of a garrison state.

Meanwhile, the repercussions from Poland on the other countries of Eastern Europe have created new problems for them as well. For a time, when Polish coal mines were virtually closed, CMEA countries had to go outside for alternative sources of coal, thereby using some of their scarce hard currency reserves. On a somewhat smaller scale the experience was repeated with respect to other imports from Poland by the CMEA countries. In addition, the Eastern European countries have been called upon in various ways to provide assistance to Poland — both in raw materials and in consumer goods. Because of the very large transfers to Poland from the USSR, the Soviet Union has also apparently found it necessary to reduce some of the various kinds of assistance it ordinarily provided to other CMEA countries,[1] as well as reducing some of its imports from them. All of these interacting consequences, along with a spreading wave of general Western concern with respect to Eastern Europe, have led to restraints on credit availability from the West for all of the CMEA countries.

The test for the Trilateral countries, in these grim circumstances, is to determine a constructive role. There is no possibility that Poland could become a center of maverick capitalism within the Soviet orbit — neither through any pressure created by Western sanctions nor through any largesse provided by a Western "Marshall Plan." The future of Poland will have to be worked out in ways consistent with her

---

[1]Paul Lewis, "As Poland's Economy Slides, Comecon Feels the Backlash," *The New York Times*, January 10, 1982, p. E4.

remaining a participating member of the CMEA group. What she probably needs, within the limits of whatever capabilities her own socialist system may have, is a plan for comprehensive reconstruction — with enough of the market elements visualized several decades ago by her distinguished economist, Oscar Lange, to be able to capture the imagination, and generate the commitment, of her now disillusioned and discouraged population. Whether or how that might happen, before Poland becomes a festering sore inside the CMEA system, is a challenge not only for Poland itself but also for both the USSR and the West.

To the extent that outside influence is responsible for the deterioration of Poland's economic capabilities, the Soviet Union must bear the heaviest responsibility; and to the extent that outside help is needed, the Soviet Union must bear the heaviest burden. Nevertheless, it is clearly in the interest of the West as well that Poland regain economic stability. The delicate task for the West is to find and follow a common and consistent approach that can help Poland attain some of the gains of "socialist renewal," without calling into question the Soviet Union's predominant role, but without forcing Poland back irretrievably into a completely *dirigiste* economic system. Perhaps something constructive may come from the series of consultations with representatives of the IMF that has been initiated following the request which Poland made in 1981 to be considered for membership in the IMF (as discussed in Section III, Part B, below).

Credits to Other CMEA Countries
The basis of the current weakness in Romania is somewhat similar to that in Poland — the recurrently surfacing problems of a society limping under the handicaps of grafting socialist forms onto an individualistic population. However, the difference is that the Government of Romania has, all along, maintained a tighter grip on the lives of its people, while exposing its economic system externally to the competitive forces of the Trilateral world. Although Romania has not always made the most efficient use of the capital borrowed from the West, her government has decided in time to curb its appetite for foreign borrowings, and has been able effectively to contain internal demands for higher living standards.

While Romania apparently suspended payments on her debt service early in 1982, in an effort to shock or coerce Western creditors into a rescheduling of overdue and maturing debt, the prospect is not really comparable with Poland. Romania managed to produce a $470 million trade surplus with the OECD countries in 1981, and is able to offer

68

partial payments in return for new concessions on debt rescheduling. Western creditors, including the IMF, some government agencies, and the banks, are in turn requiring a clearer understanding of plans underway. Romania definitely has a more promising base from which to work out some debt restructuring. Provided the Romanian Government is able to maintain the degree of relative independence in foreign relations that she has enjoyed in recent years — including membership in the International Monetary Fund — the country may after some time be re-established as creditworthy. Romania cannot soon, however, expect to borrow the additional amounts she would need to participate again, at the rate of increase of the '70s, in any sectors of the Western economies where she does have some comparative advantage in the goods she sells.

The USSR, whose debt has always been very small in relation to the volume of its trade, experienced significant reversals in 1981. Its net debt at the end of 1980 was only $10.4 billion, about the same as the net debt of East Germany or of Romania, but that reflected the offsetting of a considerably larger gross debt by sizable cash balances in Western banks. By mid-1981, the combined effect of shortfalls in its own trade balance with the West, and of disbursements to provide emergency relief for Poland, reduced its cash balances in Western banks from around $9 billion down to about $2 billion, with a resulting rise of its estimated net debt to about $17 billion. Nonetheless, the credit standings of the Gosbank and the Vneshtorg Bank remain of the highest grade, reflecting both the impeccable payments record of these institutions over the years and the Soviet Union's substantial gold reserves.

Meanwhile, estimates as of mid-1982 suggest that the Soviet Union's net hard currency reserves in foreign banks had already returned to about $8 billion as oil exports were stepped up and imports were closely controlled. The key question for the years just ahead, however, is whether the Soviets can or will subsidize Eastern Europe, in amounts which may aggregate as much as $20 to $25 billion annually, to support both the living standards and the debt service of these other countries. Compounding this problem, some analysts have suggested that the Soviet Union's own hard currency earnings from oil and gas will decline through the '80s, in real terms, even after taking account of the expected earnings from the Urengoi pipeline (whenever that may be completed).

Any immediate complications for the USSR in obtaining more credits to finance more trade, however, do not arise from any shortcomings of its own economy. Apart from political factors, hesitation by Western lenders would arise instead from concern that the USSR may become overstretched because of the widespread expectation that it will "stand behind" its CMEA partners with an "umbrella" — an expectation which Soviet officials describe as a figment of Western imaginations. Whether or not the IBEC or the IIB[1] might become sources of distress finance for Poland or Romania, or even of temporary assistance for other Eastern European countries tainted by association with them, with repercussions back upon the USSR as a principal stockholder, has yet to be tested. (The IBEC and the IIB have each been borrowers in amounts of $2 to $3 billion from commercial banks in the Euro-currency market up through 1979.)

The only clear implication of the current situation is that with respect to the USSR or the other CMEA countries the availability of more credit is the key to stimulating more trade. What this means is that the possibility of financial sanctions, which Western governments could conceivably threaten to impose on a concerted basis by directing their banks to curtail new credits, might be the most powerful lever available for exerting economic pressure on the USSR — if sanctions of any kind should be favored by a significant number of Western countries. No doubt the combined lending facilities of the Trilateral countries more nearly represent a monopolistic potential for exerting a powerful economic influence on the CMEA countries than any monopolistic controls over particular goods exported to the East that a combination of Trilateral countries would be likely to agree to impose. To repeat a homily, it may still be true, both in the West and in the East, that "money governs trade."

Yet it would be unfortunate, as well as costly, in the circumstances of 1982 if the Western governments were to direct the major Western suppliers of credit to quarantine the CMEA countries as a group — in effect inviting those countries to default on existing debt service. The economic positions of the other four East European countries — Bulgaria, Czechoslovakia, East Germany, and Hungary — as well as the credit standing of the USSR do seem capable of supporting enough additional credits to prime renewed expansion of Western trade flows to them. Whether trade and credit can be revived so far as the USSR is concerned will depend, of course, on a relaxation of political tensions.

The individual positions and performance of the others vary so widely, however, that credit may appropriately be related to the individual situations of each. Those in turn can best be judged by the suppliers of credit on the basis of the progress each country has made,

---

[1]The International Bank for Economic Cooperation (IBEC) and the International Investment Bank (IIB) are described above in Section I, Part A.

or is making, in converting its imports into added capacity for producing enough saleable exports (after providing something for the home markets) to service adequately its outstanding debt. If Western governments decide in these circumstances to discourage the further extending of credits to a particular CMEA country, that can best be done by withdrawing any existing governmental credit insurance or guarantees, and by relying on the credit suppliers themselves to exercise prudent judgments when risks are high. For Western governments to intrude further by directing lenders to deny credits as an instrument of punitive foreign policy, however, cannot be attempted very often without impairing the autonomous nature of the lending decisions made by the institutions comprising the Western financial system.

Formal Procedures of Credit Extension

If lenders are prepared to consider extending credit, there are many ways through which such credit can be, and has been, made available other than through open credit lines or uncollateralized general purpose loans from banks. To be sure, the Soviet Union has generally resisted supplier credits,[1] preferring instead the greater flexibility of bank lines. (Such a shift in the form of credit offered by the Japanese was agreed upon by Prime Minister Tanaka in negotiations with President Brezhnev as early as 1973.) But if and when trade credits or any number of varieties of bank credits come to be considered, the Trilateral countries will probably continue to make use of many of the same kinds of credit facilities which have been used in trade with the developing countries, as well as in trade among the Western countries themselves. These have on occasion, to be sure, included subsidies, which have also sometimes been accompanied by government guarantees of bank credit; or the guarantees have been substituted for subsidies.[2] As a general rule, however, the authors of this study consider credit subsidies in any form to advanced industrial countries, whether in the East or in the West, as an undesirable distortion of basic economic values.

---

[1]For example, as of the end of 1977, about 62 percent of the USSR hard currency debt represented drawings on the official credit agencies of Western governments; 25 percent was loaned by commercial banks; and only 13 percent was supplier credit, according to W.F. Kolarik, Jr., citing the Chase World Information Company, in *Issues in East-West Commercial Relations*, papers submitted to the Congressional Joint Economic Committee (U.S. Government Printing Office, 1979), p. 193.

[2]*Ibid.*, pp. 194 and 200. Western government export credit agencies had outstanding commitments to the CMEA countries of nearly $32 billion at the end of 1977, of which about $22 billion had been drawn down. Of these commitments, the USSR had received $14.2 billion; Poland, $8.3 billion. At that time, Canada's share was just under two-thirds of a billion dollars; the United States, just under a billion; while West Germany, France, and Japan were committed for, respectively, $7.5, $7, and $5 billion. Italy was committed for about $3.75 billion, and the United Kingdom, about $2 billion.

The more straightforward types of business transactions which readily attract financing are those involving two-way exchanges that are eagerly sought by both sides, such as the natural gas pipeline (which became controversial for political, not economic, reasons). There has not been such controversy in the West, moreover, in the case of the recent Japanese-Soviet contract for a forest development project, signed in June 1981, because it was clear that this did not represent a risk of vulnerable dependence; Japan's timber imports could be easily replaced from an alternate source. Japan exports the heavy equipment needed (such as bulldozers, heavy trucks, and some sawmill equipment) and imports some of the logs and lumber produced. Japanese banks provide the credit with assistance from the Japanese Export-Import Bank. All maintain close surveillance to assure that the equipment is used as intended, that it is adequately maintained, and that spare parts are available to assure continuous operation. It is through such surveillance that the Japanese meet their own requirement for being able to assess the quality of the credit by gauging the profitability of the project. While Japan does not provide concessional credit terms to the Soviet Union, the Japanese Export-Import Bank will take the later maturities of term loans, leaving the earlier maturities to the banks, which thus carry less risk. This represents, in the authors' view, the kind of credit assistance which can be appropriately provided by a government to its own nationals in facilitating foreign trade.

Most Western countries have found the IBEC and IIB to be very conservative and inflexible. While they sometimes play a role through influencing the terms set for particular loans from Western sources, no joint financing facilities have been worked out with them for sharing credits in joint construction or manufacturing projects. For example, they play virtually no role in Japan's trade with Eastern Europe. There, because no large projects comparable to those in Siberia are available, Japan's trade volume remains relatively small — consisting of such varied items as synthetic fibers, inorganic chemicals, and galvanized steel, with the financing mainly along customary commercial lines. Japanese lending is based not only on the appraisal of individual country risks (taking into account the possibility of unduly large borrowings by these countries from others) but also on the ability to relate individual loans to individually verifiable transactions, in contrast with open lines for general balance of payments purposes. In this respect, the practices of most West European and North American banks are likely to follow a similar course in the future as a consequence of the exposures that have been experienced in Poland and Romania.

Longer-Term Potentialities for CMEA Finance

What the entire CMEA group needs for a sustained expansion of East-West trade, however, is a more fluid monetary system, not only among the CMEA countries but also between them individually and the Trilateral countries. The extensive dependence on semi-barter arrangements may be approaching its practical limits, except for the USSR itself. Unless progress can be made toward using some form of ruble convertible with Western currencies, finance will become an operational limit on any substantial expansion of trade, even under the best of political environments. Hungary's contemplated intention to begin partial convertibility of the forint in 1982 is illustrative of the compelling economic force toward externalizing their currency relations that the centrally planned economies experience, as they try to extend their trade by entering markets where they may have some comparative advantage in the West.

The monetary system of the West, for all its flaws and volatility, does provide the ready convertibility among currencies which, together with a relative freedom of trade, makes possible the flourishing of mutual growth among the Western countries. To be sure, the process in the West has depended on a market system responsive to the guidance of flexible prices, providing a framework through which flows of funds can in effect integrate the economies of the Trilateral countries. But that may not be a necessary condition for the centrally planned economies; they are increasingly developing their own proxies for market pricing as they relate their own plans to the world prices outside.

Indeed in 1971 when the CMEA countries first developed the so-called "Comprehensive Program," one aim was to move beyond the confines of bilateral clearing arrangements toward a form of currency convertibility among themselves. Although the "transferable ruble" (originally created in 1964) was given broader scope in 1976, the distortions in price relationships among products persist, and the CMEA trading partners have problems agreeing on equivalent prices in terms of rubles. As a result, the CMEA countries try to have bilateral balances with each other. Where that proves too difficult they try to conduct trade with each other in hard currencies, taking little advantage of the facilities for multilateral clearing and settlement through the IBEC.

None of the CMEA countries, with the exception of Hungary, has considered experimenting with some form of convertibility between its domestic currency and the hard currencies of the West. But once Romania straightens out her currency disarray, and now that Hungary has joined her in membership in the IMF, there may be fresh opportunities for experimentation. While the particular economic and political constraints of individual CMEA countries may prevent some from trying to make their currencies convertible for limited purposes in the West, any steps taken in that direction will help to expand the zone for growing trade.

Effective integration even among the CMEA countries themselves will undoubtedly still await the instituting of a genuinely convertible ruble as the means of intra-CMEA payment, and as the currency in which temporary credits among CMEA partners are held. That is almost certain to come as they loosen up the flow of goods among themselves. The CMEA countries might then begin to develop within their own group a version of what used to prevail in the West as the "fixed parity" system — the prerequisite initial stage of the currency convertibility which promotes economic integration, as countries become able to respond more flexibly to economic incentives and pressures for specialization. This may indeed be a necessary step if the CMEA is to improve its productivity substantially. Once that begins, recognition will no doubt also grow of the need for the IBEC to exercise a monitoring role, checking any tendency for particular members to become persistent debtors or persistent creditors. Part of that adjustment will require the evolution of procedures for altering the exchange rate on occasion between a given East European currency and the ruble.

All of this, of course, is some distance ahead. But it is a likely path as the CMEA countries respond to their urgent needs for a wider diffusion of their respective capabilities, in order to gain the growth advantages of mutually profitable trade. And as intra-CMEA convertibility demonstrates the potential of each of the member countries for widening its own area for specialization, as a basis for greater trade, the advantages of moving toward a degree of convertibility between the ruble and one or more of the hard currencies of the West may become more compellingly apparent. That approach toward the economics of mutual advantage can widen further the scope for East-West trade — within whatever are the prudent limits of acceptable interdependence, and subject to the chronic shortcomings of the Eastern economic and political systems in producing exports on competitive terms.

Under such conditions, the potentialities for expansion of the East's financial facilities may be considerably enlarged within the credit and capital markets of the West. It is an interesting indication of possible room for more CMEA borrowing, within the West's diversified pattern of international lending, that the total borrowings of the CMEA countries in the international bond and Euro-currency markets in the three years 1977-79 were only 8.5 percent of the amount of borrowings in those same markets by the total of all non-oil developing countries. For the period from the beginning of 1977 through the second quarter of 1981, the CMEA credits were less than 7 percent of the credits extended in the international markets to all of the non-oil LDCs.[1] The scope for growth in such credits to the CMEA countries is thus by comparison very large indeed, provided the political and economic environment can improve during the course of the '80s.

Opportunities for expanding finance as the condition for expanding trade would be further enlarged if more external use were to be made of the IBEC and the IIB by the CMEA countries. The two banks could borrow more in their own names. They could add their guarantees to those of the individual CMEA countries for particular credits from the West. They could follow the example of the multinational regional banks in the West (the Inter-American Development Bank and the Asian Development Bank, for example) by participating with commercial banks in the joint financing of projects, thereby giving an implied degree of credit risk protection to the banking lenders. Nor is it inconceivable that the two banks, possibly along with the Soviet Union's Vneshtorg Bank, could participate as observers in the consultations organized by the OECD to consider guidelines for the terms on which export financing is made available. To be sure, none of these visionary prospects could ever materialize unless the various CMEA countries could so manage their imports as to provide for adequate service of all external debt.

While 1982 may be destined to run its course as a year of stagnation in East-West finance, as well as trade, it is in just such a period when useful consideration can be given to exploring forward possibilities. And as suggested here, there are constructive potentials which each side could appraise, during this lull, in order to be ready to take advantage of opportunities if the climate for economic relations improves. While considering these opportunities, however, the Western lenders — both governments and banks — must take care to avoid allowing political or competitive pressures to force them into uneconomic decisions, such as expanding credit on concessional terms. There is scope, to be sure, for responding to some of the Soviet legerdemain through which nominal rates of interest are kept low for appearances' sake, while appropriate real rates of interest are actually

---

[1] *Borrowing in International Capital Markets*, World Bank publication, EC 181/811, November 1981, pp. 14-15.

paid by making upward adjustments in the prices of the products for which the credit is extended. (Such concealing of interest-equivalents in the prices set for products has occurred, for example, in the negotiations for the Urengoi pipeline contracts.) Indeed, if trade is to expand on the basis of credit, the credit should not be forthcoming unless the terms (directly or indirectly) reflect the true cost of money. Fortunately, the free market system provides a natural limit on the extent to which private financial institutions can make uneconomic decisions.

III. THE REALISTIC PROSPECTS FOR TRILATERAL POLICY

The preceding section has focused on the principal sectors in which mutually profitable trade or financial transactions have occurred, and pointed to further potentials which might still be beckoning if such matters could be determined by purely economic considerations. Yet running through all of this appraisal has been the necessary recognition that economic gain must be weighed against the possible risk of compromising the political or strategic position of the West. Relations between the Trilateral countries and those of the CMEA are dominated by the underlying adversary relationship between the two superpowers, and between the political ideologies and economic systems which each represents. The climate of East-West relations can consequently never duplicate the relative consensus among the more homogeneous countries of the West in the postwar period. And that is why it would be quixotic to extrapolate for East-West economic relations any similarity to the kind of trade-propelled growth that has contributed greatly to the impressive improvement of living standards in the West over the past thirty-five years.

Nonetheless, each of the countries on both the Trilateral and the CMEA sides has experienced enough of the possible gains from wider trade relations to make worthwhile a renewed probing into the kinds of economic contact that might still be feasible in this East-West environment of an underlying adversary relationship. As essential preconditions, to be sure, the combative postures of both sides must have become restrained, and their military capabilities must be in a rough equilibrium. It has been under just such conditions, after all, that economic interrelations have grown, and at times flourished, among other potential enemy states throughout history, from the Greek city states to most European countries during the century after Napoleon. It would seem perverse, at the level of civilization that has now been reached, if the irrepressible human drive for economic gain could not be allowed some further range — within constraints set by a balancing of basic national security requirements.

Experience already has demonstrated, however, that an expansion of trade and investment relationships does not necessarily lead to an all-round lessening of tensions, and it would be naïve to presume otherwise. Because of their continuing concern over the immense growth of the Soviet military establishment, and over what is perceived as Soviet expansionism, as well as for reasons of simple prudence, the governments of the Trilateral countries have to guard against undue dependence or concentration on individual markets or suppliers in the East. This means that even the most liberally-oriented Western governments must, when their firms engage in trade with enterprises in the CMEA economies, monitor those contacts. Such general surveillance of the size and nature of private business transactions is appropriate in order to assure that, in the aggregate, the activities of all firms in a given country are consistent with its national interest in maintaining a reasonable balance between economic gain and strategic exposure for the country as a whole.

To be sure, the USSR, because of the very nature of its system, places serious limitations on the extent to which individuals from the West can personally participate, or Western firms can become directly involved, in the actual functioning of the Soviet economy. Similar though varying constraints prevail for Westerners through most economic sectors of the other six CMEA countries. In addition, all trade and financial arrangements must fit within the current economic plan of each of the CMEA countries. Still, the combination of secrecy and planning rigidity, though often frustrating, has not in the past prevented determined Western businessmen, engineers, and bankers from finding fruitful opportunities both to sell and to buy, as the data in Section I and the examples in Section II have demonstrated.

Not all business relationships have, of course, been fruitful. At some times disappointments have been the result of poor business judgment; at others, the consequence of costly delays within the CMEA bureaucracies, or misunderstandings as to terms or objectives. But often, too, the cause has been an interruption due to political events on one side or the other. To be sure, political intervention has to be expected in threatening situations, and broad political surveillance to assure suitable diversification of risks is desirable. But there is need for fuller communication among the Trilateral countries as to the aims and possible consequences of political intervention, and the mechanisms of any controls actually exercised by governments can surely be improved to avoid the stop-go-stop sequence of the past three decades. Indeed, the value of future East-West economic relations to the various countries, and the attractiveness of the prospects for individual firms, will depend upon a greater regularizing of the procedures of control, to avoid the costly adjustments for individual businesses that have been caused by the erratic implementation of controls in the past.

From the CMEA side, opportunities for advantageous economic relations have been furthered by the extent to which the CMEA governments have permitted contacts with firms of all kinds from the Trilateral countries, have expedited business negotiations, and have permitted their business executives to travel abroad. While Western governments do not restrict the personal travel of their nationals in the manner typical of the CMEA countries, nor limit access to most of their firms by CMEA nationals, two other forms of governmental control do set limits on trade originating in the West. One (see pp. 79-83) is the continuing control or prohibition under the CoCom arrangements of exports of "militarily significant goods and technology." The other (pp. 83-89) is the use of economic sanctions, as appropriate, to curb trade in order to support an urgent objective of Western foreign policy.

Following discussion of each of these boundary-setting limitations on trade, consideration in this study will shift to the positive side — the potentialities for further growth of trade in the sectors of economic activity that are outside these boundaries. Such prospects may be advanced through (pp. 90-95) promotional support by individual Western governments or through new bilateral or multilateral governmental organizations and treaties, (pp. 95-99) broader reliance on existing international institutions, and (pp. 99-101) other private sector initiatives by the Western countries.

A. POLICIES OF RESTRAINT

CoCom Controls Over Sensitive Strategic Goods and Technology[1]
As already mentioned in discussing the various sectors of existing economic relations, the Trilateral countries have agreed in principle, on a continuing basis, to prevent exports to the CMEA (and some other communist countries) of weapons and other unique military equipment, as well as particular products and technology that support military capability. The systematic management of this effort has been in operation since January 1, 1950, through the Committee for the

---

[1]The factual basis of this discussion of CoCom draws heavily on a memorandum prepared for the writers of this study by Kate S. Tomlinson and John P. Hardt, members of the Congressional Research Service of the U.S. Congress, entitled "CoCom: Conflict and Cooperation," January 25, 1982 (36 pages). All opinions or conclusions expressed in this discussion are, however, those of the authors and not the responsibility of Ms. Tomlinson or Dr. Hardt.

Control of the Export of Strategic Commodities (CoCom).[1] The fifteen participating Trilateral countries include all of the NATO members except Iceland, plus Japan (Sweden and Switzerland are not members but often cooperate informally).

The first high level (Deputy Minister) meeting of CoCom members in twenty-three years was held in Paris on January 19 and 20, 1982, in order "to review together, after more than thirty years of the Committee's existence, means to insure the adaptation of its methods to the evolution of the situation, particularly in the technological field of strategic importance."[2] Government representatives at a somewhat lower level meet each three years, however, to review basic lists of proscribed items. These fall into three categories: munitions, atomic materials, and industrial-commercial products. A permanent staff in Paris, supported by civil servants from the Paris embassies of the member countries, meets frequently to consider interpretations and exceptions. All decisions, both as to the lists and the interpretations and exceptions, must be unanimous; thus any one country can exercise a veto. The Committee itself has no legal status but exists on the basis of a gentlemen's agreement. For that reason it has no enforcement powers of its own; all enforcement is the responsibility of each member country.

Even with its relatively large membership, and with a reasonably good record of voluntary compliance and enforcement, CoCom has been limited in its ability to insulate the CMEA countries from advances in Western military materiel, or to deny them access to sophisticated civilian technology capable of improving the CMEA military potential. Nonetheless, CoCom does set a borderline, outside of which most Western concerns may feel relatively free to operate, and to develop broader trading opportunities. Understandably, however, there are problems at the margins, partly because many of the precise terms of CoCom lists and interpretations are secret, making it difficult for a business firm to know in advance whether a proposed transaction will be allowed. Indeed, the further one looks into the actual implementation of CoCom, even its comparatively straightforward role in setting a military-defense borderline between forbidden and permitted trade becomes complicated.

One major area in which the United States has been urging CoCom to strengthen its controls is the transfer of technology in the form of

---

[1]Because it is only an informal agreement among the participating governments, CoCom has no formal official title and is known by a variety of titles, including the "Consultative Group Coordination Committee."

[2]CoCom press release of January 21, 1982.

licenses, designs, and technical information, in order to supplement the existing control over the sale of end-products. Though limiting technological products as such is clearly of particular significance and relevance in meeting CoCom's objectives, the actual implementing of controls over scientific and engineering processes poses even greater problems of interpretation and monitoring, requiring highly skilled technical expertise. Tighter controls will, for example, heighten the concern already expressed by many firms and some countries that they risk exposure of proprietary information on their manufacturing processes and product designs through the CoCom system.

Problems arise also from the existing practice of applying somewhat less stringent, or more widely varying, standards to exports destined for the Eastern European countries, as contrasted with the more rigid approach to exports to the Soviet Union. Risks of slippage arise not only through transshipment among CMEA countries but also because of variations in interpretation among the CoCom countries. These risks are increasing as more CoCom restraints are applied to dual-use items, capable of serving either civilian or military uses.

The question of gauging whether a product could be devoted to a significant military capability would be further complicated if a criterion recently suggested in Congressional testimony by an American official should be adopted. He implied a readiness to move back toward the U.S. standards of 1962-69, which have since been rejected, but which then aimed at limiting "economic" as well as "military" development. His suggestion was that restrictions should now apply to products "which contribute significantly to the industrial infrastructure which supports military production."[1] Other commentators, particularly in the United States, have suggested going even further to affect "military capability" by trying through extensive controls to reduce the economic and political stability of the CMEA.

The further back into a potential adversary's economy that the restrictions are extended, the less precise they are likely to be, and the less susceptible to uniform understanding and compliance by the CoCom members. As demonstrated in recent experience, the West Europeans clearly disagree with tendencies in the United States to extend CoCom into continuing controls over a broad range of products and processes. They stress their much closer geographical and

---

[1] Robert D. Hormats, Assistant Secretary of State for Economic and Business Affairs, Testimony before the Subcommittee on Economic Policy and Trade, House Committee on Foreign Affairs, November 12, 1981, p. 10. While the Department of State subsequently modified this position, the U.S. Department of Defense has continued to press for even stricter controls over a broad range of "infrastructure" transactions.

historical affinity in trading relations with the East, and their greater potential for significant economic gains through two-way trade. For such reasons, it seems quite unlikely that an agreed and effective approach along the broader lines favored by some in the United States could be worked out. If broadening were attempted, that might even impair CoCom's effectiveness within the narrower boundaries set by present procedures. While the United States Government will undoubtedly continue to apply tighter standards to its own nationals, the actual effectiveness of such measures will be limited.

When centered on the concept of denying strictly military hardware, or immediately relevant and significant technology, it should be possible to develop reasonably workable criteria. For borderline cases, or with respect to newly emerging technologies, which should be proscribed until they become too widespread to be effectively controllable, reliance will have to be placed more heavily on the quality of the review procedure rather than upon the formulation of voluminous and inflexible lists and product specifications. Such a review process will have to be eclectic, and should be conducted by a competent, permanent staff of highly specialized scientists and engineers, working under the overall guidance of political officials. The review should take into consideration not only an exported product as such, but also the technology embodied within it, the use to which it is to be put, and the practical likelihood of diversion to purposes that would significantly advance military capabilities.

To be sure, in addition to the definitional problems of distinguishing acceptable from unacceptable close substitutes, it will always be difficult to maintain fully effective control over flows out of an open society. Greater strength would be imparted to the effort, however, if the participating countries could endow CoCom with a firm legal status by establishing a formal organization, preferably through international treaties. Such treaties should lay out the principles guiding the cooperation of members in monitoring and regulating transactions which may affect national security. They should not, however, attempt to establish detailed operating procedures, nor even to specify the target countries. If that were combined with an operating emphasis on selecting a relatively small set of very critical items, CoCom might reduce the risks of evasion or loss of credibility that would be created by casting a wide dragnet.

In this sense, to maintain an effective CoCom procedure, year in and year out, should be a primary objective of the Trilateral countries. The reference marker should be military relevance, however, and not simply the determination of one or more of the Trilateral countries to chastise the USSR or other CMEA countries for current foreign policy purposes. By comparison, the economic sanctions to be described next can at best serve only very limited purposes, while the CoCom approach offers the possibility of an ongoing unity of commitment. Such an approach, by inference, creates for the businesses initiating trading ventures a more stable and less ambiguous zone of opportunity for the development of mutually advantageous economic relations with the East.

The Western Use of Economic Sanctions

Recourse to economic sanctions has a long history as an instrument of foreign policy. Despite the impressions of much of the general public, however, sanctions are not initiated by governments with the aim of directly crippling another nation's military capabilities. Instead, they are usually employed as an instrument of political leverage intended to reinforce other diplomatic maneuvers, or to modify or influence another nation's behavior in future situations. Sanctions may include an embargo, a boycott, a blockade, or a partial form of any of these, or the revocation of trading privileges (such as Most Favored Nation status), or the imposition of punitive regulations or of controls over the granting of credits, or the blockage or restricting of assets. They may be imposed by one country or by many.

In general, to exert an effective impact, however, sanctions must significantly affect the sources of whatever product or process is to be restricted; must be sustained with reasonable consistency; must affect the opponent in a critically vital sector; and should present the opponent with a realistic choice, that is, one that the opponent has the power to deliver or fulfill. While economic in nature, sanctions do not call for an economic reaction but are intended instead to convey an emphatic political message. Sanctions are probably most effective as a foreign policy instrument if they are used simply as a threat, without having to be actually exercised. That requires, of course, a substantial degree of credibility, which depends upon the opponent believing that the sanctions can in fact be exercised by an effective number of participants, and that they would inflict real punishment or damage. The sanctions actually used, or threatened, may not necessarily even affect trade directly, since the restriction of access to credit may in some circumstances be the more powerful instrument.

As invoked by the United Nations against Rhodesia, for example, sanctions may have hampered exports and imports somewhat, creating internal economic strains that might have helped support the eventual change to the new Government of Zimbabwe, but the pattern was surely not one of uniform or regular compliance by all countries. American sanctions against Iran, centering on blocking financial assets, but including an embargo on all exports except food, clothing, and medicines, may have helped precipitate the release of American hostages. But the conditions were unusual, and the objective clear-cut. A principal architect of those arrangements has concluded, in attempting to draw meaningful implications from the Iranian experience, that "there is little the United States can do unilaterally [through economic sanctions] that would visit economic punishment on the USSR." He concludes in the same analysis that none of the United States' economic sanctions in the past — against North Korea, the People's Republic of China, Cuba, North Vietnam, and Cambodia — have achieved any significant foreign policy objective.[1]

As invoked by the United States against the Soviet Union's movement of troops into Afghanistan at the end of 1979, the aim of the sanctions was both symbolic and substantive. The United States sought to dramatize its disapproval of the Soviet move, and it sought to physically punish the Soviets by forcing them to slaughter livestock as grain shipments dropped, thereby ultimately reducing Soviet meat production. While it was not the expectation of the U.S. Administration, there was a vain hope by some Americans that the Soviet troops might then be withdrawn, particularly if votes of condemnation in the United Nations could be backed by a widespread use of substantive sanctions by other countries to reinforce those of the United States.

In practice, at a conference of grain exporters early in 1980, Canada, Australia, and the European Economic Community, without actually reducing their grain sales, did agree to hold their exports to the USSR at "normal" or "traditional" levels. Argentina, for grain and soybeans, and Brazil, for soybeans, declined to cooperate in the embargo but did pledge not to take commercial advantage of the U.S. action — a pledge that was not fulfilled. Beyond grain, Japan was the only other major participant in the sanctions; she agreed to a general curbing of commercial exports. Others undertook symbolic action, or simply indicated an intention not to replace with their exports the goods being embargoed by the United States. Most other exports to the Soviet Union from the Trilateral countries continued, or increased, during 1980. In overall terms, while United States exports to the Soviet Union

---

[1]Robert Carswell, "Economic Sanctions and the Iranian Experience," *Foreign Affairs*, Winter 1981-82, pp. 260-264. Mr. Carswell was Deputy Secretary of the U.S. Treasury from early 1977 to January 1981. See also Benno Engels, *Die Zukunft des Embargos in den Internationalen Beziehungen* (Hamburg: 1981), pp. 7-11.

declined by nearly $2 billion from 1979 to 1980, exports by the remaining OECD countries to the Soviet Union increased by over $4 billion.

The outcome of the partial grain embargo was a boomerang — inflicting more economic damage on the United States than the Soviet Union (Section II, Part B, above) — even though President Reagan lifted the ban before the full marketing of the 1980/81 crop had been completed. During 1981 not only Argentina and Brazil but also Canada, the European Economic Community, and even Sweden (which does not normally export grain) sold all they had available to the Soviet Union, while the United States lost a substantial portion of its market share. The most succinct summary of the overall impact of the Afghanistan sanctions was made by the head of the U.S. Department of Agriculture's Eastern Europe/Soviet Branch, Anton Malish, in saying, "The last embargo caused the Soviets some difficulties that were more than trivial, but basically, they just amount to nuisances." Or as one of his colleagues said more colorfully, "We really shot ourselves in the foot with that one."[1]

The impact of sanctions has at times been experienced more as a fragmentation within the Western alliance than as a punishment for the East. Such an outcome is typically illustrated by the Novolipetsk Dynamo Steel Project in the Soviet Union. Armco, Inc. (U.S.), formerly the Armco Steel Co., and Nippon Steel (Japan) had decided in April 1976 to work together to obtain a contract for equipment in this proposed plant designed to produce 500,000 tons per year of electrical steel — using technology developed initially by Armco but also licensed to Nippon. After more than four years of negotiation, involving almost monthly trips to the USSR by various experts, and the compiling of many volumes of specifications, and after tentatively arranging financial support from the Japanese Export-Import Bank, the two firms prepared an 8000-page final contract in consultation with Soviet representatives. By December 1979 Armco had obtained virtually all of the needed U.S. export licenses for its part of the project, and the contract was signed on December 17. On January 11, 1980, following the Soviet move into Afghanistan, the United States suspended the export licenses, and in April the USSR responded by terminating the contract. At the same time, Japan announced its intention to control the extension of credit to the Soviet Union and to delay negotiations over other major projects. Soon thereafter, Creusot-Loire (France), which had led a major competing group over the four years of prior negotiation, was awarded a contract for roughly comparable equipment which did not,

---

[1]"Banning Trade with Soviets is Questioned," *The Wall Street Journal*, December 22, 1981, p. 23.

however, have the full technical capability of the Armco-Nippon design. Supportive financing was also provided. The technical difference in grades of finished product between the Armco-Nippon and the Creusot-Loire installations was noted by the French Government as justification for its view that there had been no violation of the understanding that French companies would not fill any void left by the imposition of U.S. sanctions against the USSR.

Nonetheless, the United States under the Reagan Administration has set about trying to influence both Soviet and Polish behavior, since the martial law regime began in Poland, by again imposing sanctions, though this time of a much more selective and limited scope. The United Kingdom took action deliberately intended as merely symbolic, at first, and thus of little immediate cost at home or to the Soviets or to the Poles; the Common Market announced limited sanctions; but there was no general agreement on whether any kind of trade embargo could help the lifting of martial law and a recovery of Poland to economic health. There has indeed been reason to fear that an embargo might be counterproductive, forcing Poland into a permanently *dirigiste* system at reduced living standards, while the Soviet-style economic autarky of the '50s is renewed among the CMEA countries.

Whatever else the ultimate result of the most recent attempts to exert leverage on Soviet (and Polish) action may be, the use of sanctions has in any event crippled for some time to come any return toward the expansion of U.S.-Soviet trade that had occurred through the 1970s. These moves have also placed new hurdles in the path of East-West trade and investment for most other CMEA and Trilateral countries. The U.S. sanctions, with scattered support from other Trilateral countries, have also given new impetus on the Soviet side toward a broader diversification of its own trade and commitments across the world.

Against this current background, and the experience thus far through two rounds of sanctions, the longer term issue for the West is whether to regard sanctions for the future as a more-or-less normal instrument of foreign policy, available for intermittent use, or whether the costs so often outweigh the gains that any attempt to exert pressure in the relationships between East and West should, with only rare exceptions, be shunted away from economic sanctions and toward traditional diplomacy.

What are the costs for the countries that impose economic sanctions? Most immediately, companies in those countries lose what were presumably profitable sales (unless governments provide some offsetting compensation). Moreover, having thereby become unreliable suppliers, they stand to lose future business opportunities, with possible adverse implications for the country's employment, growth, and balance of payments. And unless the sanctioning country embargoes all sales and purchases by its own firms to or from the target countries, domestic problems will arise from the uneven internal distribution of the burden created by the sanctions among exporting sectors of the economy. Since there will be important domestic sectors bearing no direct burden at all, complaints will arise over the need to shift some of the burden, in effect, to them. Beyond that, unless all other countries apply sanctions in parallel, firms in a sanction-imposing country simply lose market share to competitors in another country — while the impact on the target country is at most a matter of inconvenience, and possibly some delay, as the goods, or the technology, are eventually delivered despite the sanctions.

These are the first-line costs, quantifiable to some degree. Behind these are the intangible costs of conflict and disarray among allies. Judgments will inevitably vary among countries as to the political need for punitive action, its timing, its comprehensiveness, and its probable leverage effect. Such differences will be aggravated, too, by more mundane material considerations as some countries have much heavier involvements (and higher opportunity costs) than others in their economic relations with a target country. At the least, to minimize friction there should be advance consultation, prompt but genuine, both when sanctions are being put on and when they are taken off. Moreover, unless some agreed and reasonably equitable procedure for sharing or redistributing the burdens and costs among participating countries is worked out in advance, their unity of action is not likely to persist for long. There need not, of course, be unanimity among the allies in all actions taken or contemplated; that would be a virtual impossibility. But there must be enough agreement among enough allies to assure the registering of a meaningful message. And that should, if at all possible, rest upon a lasting, general consensus among the principal allies on the broad purposes of, and principles applicable to, the use of sanctions.

Without advance consultation — which did not occur when the United States moved against the USSR in the case of Afghanistan — cleavages of wide-ranging significance develop among allies. In the end, this fragmentation was counterproductive to the U.S. effort, as the actual sanctions were matched only in part, and only by some of the allies. Those who did participate were chagrined when the United States later removed its principal sanction (on grain) without consultation. The Soviet Union, however, was apparently not seriously affected; the gain from an American point of view was that the intensity of its disapproval was unambiguously expressed. More subtly, though, the prestige of the United States as a skilled and effective leader of the Trilateral world was tarnished.

In contrast with most experience thus far, the potential gains from sanctions might conceivably be more than merely to gratify a frustrated urge to "do something." For a tightly maintained trade embargo — if enforced comprehensively with the commitment and sacrifice comparable to that which allies would undertake in the event of actual warfare — or even the threat of such an embargo, could exert powerful leverage. The pressure might be great enough, at least to force the initiation of negotiations concerning a possible settlement, particularly on a relatively clear-cut issue. Another conceivably effective approach would be a total embargo of just one or two absolutely essential items, such as grain, assuming such an embargo could be effectively maintained. Similarly, the cutting off of additional credits might help to nudge an adversary to the conference table.

The power of concerted sanctions would be greater as the adversary is smaller, however. The prospect of effectively using economic leverage to force an actual capitulation of the USSR (or the CMEA), or even to exert a determining impact on the outcome of negotiations, seems remote indeed when stripped of emotional urges and considered in cold logic. Experience has shown that the Soviet Union is generally better able than the West to withstand economic strains while pursuing political ends. The best hope is that just the threat of sanctions, if carefully planned, widely supported, and accompanied by commitments to share the burdens of lost markets, could at times of acute tension bring about discussions which diplomacy alone might not otherwise have been able to initiate. To paraphrase the words of one Soviet official consulted during the preparation of this study, "The USSR can never be pushed by an ultimatum, or a public display of pressure; we do understand the use of pressure in quiet negotiations."

Despite their potential costs, sanctions have continued to appeal to human nature as an expression of force without warfare. The temptation to resort to sanctions or economic leverage may occur as often in the East as in the West, when preponderant economic advantage permits their consideration. So long as adversary relationships persist between the Trilateral and the CMEA countries, economic sanctions will remain a lurking possibility, and will in that sense set a kind of boundary of mistrust upon the expansion of trade. But it is an elastic boundary, which every country on either side will have to determine for itself. That is, each will have to gauge for itself the extent to which it can afford to be dependent on the other side as a market for exports or as a source of needed imports. For the Western nations, such a decision should be made in the light of the alternatives in the event of a trade interruption. Such alternatives could be broadened through advance consultation and contingency planning. In any event, while considering its own participation in sanctions, each nation will become keenly aware of the problem identified by the former United States Secretary of State, Dean Rusk:

> During the post-war decades...many of us tended to think of trade as a 'favor' which we were doing for someone else. That attitude is [now] a luxury....We must turn the question around and ask ourselves what ought to be the policies and practices which justify denying ourselves the benefits of trade in a tumultuous and diverse world.[1]

Clearly, the sanctions of the '80s have already imposed enough cost and disarray in the West to call for a stepping back and reappraisal by the Trilateral countries. It would certainly be constructive if ways could be found to avoid the confusion which has characterized the spontaneous headlong rushes by the United States into sanctions which its allies have been unable fully to support — and which became rather futile without widespread participation. Surely anything that could be done in the West to clarify the "rules of the contest" would also provide a firmer base for commitments by those firms that see attractive and permissible business prospects in the East.

The need is for a coordinated plan of approach, considering in advance the kinds of conditions which most countries agree could justify the imposition of deliberate restraints on CMEA trade, and evaluating the kinds of sanctions that could be effectively exercised. Perhaps as an extension of a more formal organization such as that suggested in this study to strengthen the CoCom procedures, and taking an example from the International Energy Agency, the participating countries could try to agree on the kinds of thresholds at which some consultation and action would be triggered, and on the arrangements that might then be appropriate for burden-sharing among the participants when sanctions became costly. It is worth pondering whether the ability of the West simply to develop a consensus on a framework for the use of sanctions might not, by its very existence, become a powerful force for bringing about negotiations in crisis periods, thereby averting a triggering of the actual use of sanctions.

---

[1]Cited by Arthur T. Downey, "The Export Administration Act of 1979: ...," *Proceedings of the Southwestern Legal Foundation, 1980*, pp. 307-8, referring to Secretary Rusk's testimony in 1978 before the Senate Committee on Banking, Housing, and Urban Affairs.

B. POLICIES TO PROMOTE EXPANSION
OF ECONOMIC RELATIONS

If the Trilateral countries take advantage of the current hiatus in trade development to strengthen CoCom, and concert their approaches to the use of sanctions, it will become possible to think again of expanding trade along useful lines during the decade of the '80s. Paralleling a refurbishing of the Trilateral policies of precautionary restraint, constructive approaches can also be considered by the Trilateral countries for assisting the resumption of trade expansion, within the restraints of prudence, whenever more trade becomes possible. The possibilities to consider would include: 1) government initiatives which might facilitate or encourage trade with the CMEA countries; 2) the ways in which existing international institutions might help to provide conditions supportive of East-West trade expansion; and 3) the potentials which might then be activated by private initiatives within the Trilateral countries.

Governmental Initiatives to Encourage Trade

Once the boundaries of prudence are agreed upon, a number of opportunities can be pursued. Many of the more interesting opportunities for governments to assist in the expansion of East-West trade are likely to be developed unilaterally or bilaterally rather than multilaterally because the individual countries on both sides differ so widely in resources, procedures, and capabilities. Yet it would not be practical in this study to work with a matrix containing all possible separate actions, or bilateral combinations between each of the Trilateral and CMEA countries. Instead there will be, first, an outline of the unilateral or bilateral actions which have been or might be undertaken by some governments, and then, second, an identification of some constructive multilateral possibilities. Third will be a discussion of the principal multilateral need on the Western side — that is, the need for a more orderly resolving of differences in approach among Western governments.

Unilateral or Bilateral Initiatives

Each Western country, after taking account of CoCom limitations, must be able to permit or promote the trade of its own firms with any of the CMEA countries within limits determined by its own interests and its responsibility to its allies — that is, within limits determined by the aims of its diplomacy and by the degree of economic interdependence it can accept, and by its commitments to international trade agreements. For most Western countries, there would seem to be rather compelling reasons for enjoying the benefits of expanding trade with the East, so long as each has a secure fallback position at home and with its allies in case the trade is interrupted. Conversely, no single Trilateral country, including the United States, can expect that even the complete cessation of its own trade or of credit extension with the USSR would be powerful enough to stop any inclinations or capabilities the USSR might have for pursuing policies at home or abroad which the West might consider undesirable. There are simply too many other suppliers and buyers around the modern world for the trade of any one country to have a controlling significance for the USSR or the CMEA as a whole. Unilateral government actions can help promote trade, as the discussion of governmentally guaranteed credits has suggested in Section II, but such governmental actions cannot conversely be used effectively as instruments of economic warfare.

Unilateral initiatives to clear the way for productive specialization through trade usually reflect some form of bilateral understanding, such as a trade agreement between a Trilateral and a CMEA country that indicates prospective annual targets for two-way trade over a period of several years. Supported by such an agreement, most Western countries unilaterally either extend guarantees to their own firms to promote production or employment which they particularly wish to encourage, or sell their firms risk insurance to cover some part of their trade. Sometimes, as in the case of the U.S.-USSR long-term agreement on grain sales, government commitments may cover only one category of commodities and may set minimum assured availabilities. The United States Government also provides guarantees to American banks which finance sales from government-controlled stocks, but it does not enter into the negotiation of any of the contractual details — leaving that instead to the individual trading concerns and the CMEA buying agencies.

Another broad approach toward expediting bilateral exchanges is provided by establishing joint trade councils or commissions. In the case of the USSR and the United States there are, for example, two such bodies: one, at the official level, is the U.S.-USSR Economic Commission which is chaired by Cabinet Ministers from each country and includes only government officials; the other, the U.S.-USSR Trade and Economic Council, is composed on the U.S. side entirely of members from the private sector interested in trade and finance with the Soviet Union, has permanent offices in New York and Moscow, and is co-chaired by a leading American businessman and a prominent Soviet official in a trading organization. Similarly, West Germany has

91

established a bilateral trade council known as the German-Soviet Economic Commission, plus other groups, such as the Commission of the Federal Republic of Germany and the USSR for Economic, Scientific and Technical Cooperation. Comparable high level councils, of varying scope and composition, have been organized between most Trilateral and CMEA countries. Such organizations can play a significant expediting role in identifying opportunities and in calling official attention to problems.

In addition to these consultative groups, there are a large number of specific agreements for scientific, technical, and industrial cooperation. There could potentially be many more agreements between specialized organizations in CMEA countries and trade associations or individual firms in the West to serve as umbrellas under which specific business transactions could be negotiated. One complication arises from the fact that some Western countries, such as the United States, do not offer equality of treatment among all of the CMEA countries with respect to goods entering the home market. For example, while there is sometimes, with the exception of very high tariff items, more symbolism than substance in granting Most Favored Nation (MFN) treatment to CMEA countries, it is certainly a source of friction that the United States provides MFN access to Poland, Hungary, and Romania, but not to the Soviet Union, East Germany, Czechoslovakia, or Bulgaria. The United States regards MFN as a valuable privilege and continues to hold it in abeyance with respect to the USSR pending the resolution of other contested issues, such as the right of Soviet citizens to emigrate. Most other Western countries, however, do make MFN available to the goods of most CMEA countries as a matter of course.

Multilateral Possibilities
Multilateral approaches open other alternatives for the future — some based on arrangements already underway, such as those mentioned in Section II above with respect to energy, agriculture, and finance, for example, and some hinged on existing international organizations. In addition, there are a number of bilateral or multilateral projects which governments have encouraged that could spin off new opportunities for expanded trade relations over the years ahead. Examples of these include East-West cooperation in space exploration, Japanese-USSR joint activities in cultivating fisheries, multinational approaches to geophysical questions, the treaty on multinational cooperation in the Antarctic, and the U.N. agreements on the law of the sea.

In time, governments may also wish to widen the scope for joint East-West participation in the economic programs of developing countries. As visionary as such a prospect seems, in light of the hostility each side displays as to the presumed aims of the other for political liaison with the developing nations, a start has actually been made. There is already, for example, a Hungarian-Swiss-Nigerian pharmaceutical company. And companies from eight countries of East and West have joined the Government of Guinea in the Miferque Nimba Mining Company.[1] Such multilateral programs can conceivably tend to reduce politically destabilizing East-West competition while providing economic gains to all parties.

Resolving Western Differences of Approach to "Normal" Trade
Beyond the possibilities of the kind just mentioned, the overriding need on the Western side is for a more orderly approach toward resolving (or at least better managing) differences among Western governments as to the stance and the spirit of their economic relations with the USSR and Eastern Europe — outside the boundaries set by CoCom or the approach to sanctions. Such differences include disagreements over what constitutes trade subsidy, or credit subsidy, or what the guidelines as to vulnerability might be. Of course, military and economic considerations are unavoidably intermingled when such questions are faced head-on. And the only certainty is that there is not now, and probably never can be, a single, comprehensive, lasting resolution of these issues. They must be met instead through a procedure, not a formula. The premise of that procedure should be that no one country — in the tangled world of differences in performance, tradition, and capacity among the Trilateral countries — can presume to think and decide for all. Indeed, in today's interdependent Western world, no one nation should make decisions without consultation, on any issues that have a significant bearing on all.

The precursor of a new approach has to be a forthright recognition of some basic conceptual differences. As a general condition, except under a regime of sanctions or in time of actual war, the presumption in most European countries is that for their own nationals trade is a right, to be conditioned only by the legal requirements for equitable business practice and by each government's international treaty obligations. In contrast with the United States, but not going as far as Japan, there is an

---

[1]Malkevich, *op. cit.*, suggests that there were 130 tripartite cooperation agreements in operation in the mid-1970s, but mentions only these two.

assumption in the countries of Western Europe that governments will assist in opening trade opportunities. Subject only to domestic political constraints, European governments tend to resolve doubts on the side of more trade rather than less. That is a logical outgrowth of their greater dependence on trade with others, through which they expect to gain the specialization and comparative advantage of access to broader markets than their own.

Japan has, in her remarkable economic performance since World War II, emphasized diversified exports of manufactured goods and the import of raw materials; she is also clearly a trade-dependent nation. The United States, however, has been in transition from a largely self-sufficient home market with a trade component of 3 or 4 percent of GNP in the '50s, to a market with roughly 10 percent of its GNP embodied in merchandise trade in the '80s (and the percentage becomes even higher when services are included). Public understanding of the importance of two-way trade in the American economy has lagged behind the underlying structural change.

As the United States, despite her much greater size and internal diversification, moves closer to the focus on the importance of trade that is characteristic of her allies, she should also be closer to accepting some of the other conditions of interdependence: that the United States cannot maintain a position of decision-making hegemony over her allies; that a variety of existing or new procedures or institutions will increasingly have to be used to reach jointly determined approaches to issues of common interest; and that in questions of trade with the East, a common meeting ground is needed not only for CoCom problems, and for the development of a more unified approach to the possible use of sanctions, but also for considering together the attitudes and interests of each other concerning both the potentials and the risks of widening the scope of "normal" trade.

The markets and the materials available in the Soviet Union and throughout the CMEA countries are too large and varied to be ignored as the Trilateral countries reach out for new economic opportunities. Nor can the risks be ignored of any growing Eastern economic leverage on certain aspects of Western trade. Moreover, the evaluation of both gains and risks depends on a full grasp not only of their relevance to each Western country involved, but also of their combined impact on the West as a whole. That is why the issues of "normal" East-West trade cannot be settled by Summit meetings alone, whether these include five, or seven, or fifteen or more heads of government.

These are issues that require detailed ongoing assessment of the economic and political gains and risks, as seen both by the firms

94

directly involved and by government officials. To achieve a perspective suitable to the world environment of the '80s and beyond requires a framework within which the interests of each country are brought to the serious attention of the others. And that implies fuller reliance on the many competent technical staffs scattered throughout the private and public sectors of the Western countries.

While much could be done on an *ad hoc* basis toward reconciling divergent policies among a few leading countries — and certainly should be actively pursued where possible — a more permanent mechanism might well be established specifically for the review of issues arising from the differing approaches of the individual Trilateral countries to the expansion of trade and credit with the East. This might be done by augmenting the CoCom operational group, or perhaps by creating a new group under the aegis of the OECD. In any case, the counterpart of such a staff function should be regular high level review (and debate) by leading officials, with an opportunity for the hearing of representative business groups at some stage in the process.

The Scope for International Institutions
Since the boundaries set by CoCom are a precondition for the expansion of Western trade with the East, questions arise as to whether its procedures should not be more clearly institutionalized on the basis of formal treaties. Several countries for internal political reasons shy away from that, or from the binding effect of any other approach that would officially establish CoCom as a legal obligation. As already suggested, however, the time has come for reconsideration and further action to establish an independent institution, in which all fifteen CoCom countries would be participating members, and for which there should be some form of common involvement beyond the present gentlemen's agreement.

A number of existing institutions already play a positive role in facilitating the expansion of East-West trading and financing activities. The GATT, for example, includes Czechoslovakia (inactive), Hungary, Poland, and Romania in its membership. While the GATT has been struggling with the elusive problems raised by non-tariff barriers, it does provide a valuable forum and procedure for countries to resolve discriminatory trade practices. As and if Western trade grows with the state-controlled economies of the East, there will be increasingly frequent allegations of subsidies or dumping, or other practices or misunderstandings threatening the continuity of trade. The GATT can serve as a release valve for such pressures and can preside over the settlement of claims for compensation. If the United States and those other

GATT members which do not extend MFN status to some CMEA countries should eventually decide to make MFN available (presumably in the context of a broader negotiation), the usefulness to both sides of CMEA membership in GATT might become compelling. Under those conditions, the GATT forum could provide a convenient multilateral framework for resolving the differences over trading practices that are certain to arise. Moreover, association by the CMEA countries with the various GATT codes could also be helpful.

The GATT's sister organization, the IMF, may offer even more potential for aiding the development of East-West economic relations. So far as Western countries are concerned, the IMF can and should monitor the lending by its members to CMEA countries. It should be able to alert the officials of lending countries when the cumulative effect of their individual actions has been to build an alarmingly heavy aggregate of indebtedness by any one CMEA country to the West. The scope for constructive IMF influence will become much greater, of course, when and if other East European countries follow Romania and Hungary into actual IMF membership. For those who become members, the IMF can serve broader purposes than the IBEC, which has contributed very little to the multilateralizing of CMEA trade and is essentially intended as a clearing account for multilateral settlements among the CMEA countries. As the trade of the East with the West grows, there will be more and more situations in which a backstop of available and usable currencies could help smooth the flow of exports and imports, and avoid lurches between feast and famine in exchanges with the West. Indeed, with trade growing under an IMF aegis, there is scope for creating the kind of operational integration between the CMEA countries and the West that can enable the two kinds of economic systems to work effectively together — without impairing the unique identities of either. Nor, in such circumstances, would the political alignment of the Eastern countries be impinged any more than it has been for any of the 146 existing members of the IMF, whose political integrity is not questioned.

The IMF can be useful in other ways. Hungary, for example, in applying for membership in the IMF in 1981, did not foresee any actual need to borrow; but its central bank officials did look forward to partial convertibility of the forint during 1982.[1] In taking such a step there could be unforeseeable problems, possibly even a temporary run on

---

[1]Hungary became the 146th member of the IMF on May 6, 1982. By the time of its entry it had already experienced a drain on its hard currency reserves earlier in 1982, brought on by the repercussions of the Polish situation. The BIS assembled in April some $210 million of central bank credits to backstop the forint, and the IMF can henceforth be regarded as a fallback support for those credits.

the forint as a wary world tested the strength of Hungary's new resolve by withdrawing credits or deposits in hard currency. In that event, by drawing other currencies promptly from the IMF, Hungary would be able to support the forint through its transition period. Indeed, the mere knowledge in the world's markets that such drawing rights were available to the Hungarian authorities might prevent an initial run from occurring.

In the case of Poland, which has also applied to the IMF, the long-run advantages of IMF membership for repairing its standing as a debtor, and for equipping it to become a viable trading partner within the CMEA and with the West, are obvious. But Poland cannot become qualified to join the IMF without initiating structural changes in its economy, restoring conditions of normal output and trade, meeting the interest costs on its outstanding debt, and finding creditors to take over debts that are maturing. It is such conditions, however, that point toward the suggestion made in Section II that it would be critically useful to have a tacit Soviet-Western recognition of the helpful poten-tialities in an independent appraisal of Poland's economic situation and requirements. Whether carried out unostentatiously by a group from the IMF, or by any other organization or *ad hoc* group experienced in providing economic advice to governments, the hope would be that the Polish Government would, as a result, initiate needed changes within its own socialist system of production and distribution, includ-ing the providing of incentives for the Polish people.

Although most of the USSR assistance to Poland has been in the form of concessional pricing, or outright grants in aid, it has also made some Polish loans and is currently supplementing its aid-in-kind with hard currency loans for the purchase of food in the West. As such aid enables Poland to apply other earnings to its debt service — without compromising the basic Soviet position that it does not provide an "umbrella" over CMEA debts — that helps to clear the way for the West to revive some trade with Poland and extend the maturities of the outstanding debt.[1] On the basis of such understanding with the USSR and the West, the Polish Government should be able to restore the societal environment, and the personal incentives, needed for eco-nomic revival. That is the kind of development that could, in time, equip Poland to qualify for IMF membership.[2]

---

[1]All delinquent interest payments for 1981 were paid by March 1982, and debt maturing in 1981 was extended after token payments against principal. A succeeding round of negotiations for the interest and debt coming due in 1982 is underway as this study is concluded.

[2]As of May 1982, at the invitation of the Polish Government, the IMF had sent a second of its teams to Poland to conduct preliminary discussions.

This is one possible approach, but there are others, not necessarily mutually exclusive. The Bank for International Settlements might, for example, play a role in Poland's financial rehabilitation, perhaps providing, if informally requested both by the Polish authorities and by Poland's creditors, an independent mission of economic advisers to consult with the Polish Government. BIS involvement would also conveniently bring Switzerland (which is not a member of the IMF) into the process of alleviating the Polish crisis alongside other leading Western countries. Moreover, all of the CMEA countries except the USSR and East Germany are already BIS members, although none presently serve on the Governing Board. In the event that the United States should for a time prefer punitive to promotive measures, thereby possibly limiting the IMF's flexibility, the BIS (where the United States is only an observer and not a member) might initiate the organizing on the Western financial side of an acceptable relief and recovery program for Poland, once changes in the government's economic program warrant such support.

Quite apart from the current crisis, however, the BIS does serve as a useful meeting ground where the central bankers of East and West, whose language has much more in common than that of political or military officials, can meet for professional discussion of those basic problems of money and credit that are very much the same everywhere. It was in the atmosphere and understanding characteristic of the BIS that arrangements were made to shield Hungary against the initial repercussions of the Polish debt problems in early 1982. The established reputation of the BIS for integrity and neutrality between East and West should make it an ideal catalyst for advancing economic relations between both sides.

The OECD might also have a variety of constructive roles to play if the general atmosphere of tension between East and West were to lessen, and the growth of East-West trade were to be resumed. Its International Energy Agency could, for example, become the Western voice exploring further potentials for energy collaboration with the CMEA countries. If permissible exchanges of technology increase, outside the boundaries set by CoCom, the specialized staff of the OECD concerned with the parameters of such exchanges among Western countries, including the protection of patent or proprietary interests, could establish closer working relations with such Eastern bodies as the USSR Committee on Science and Technology. Such relations, for which limited beginnings had been made during the '70s, could possibly lead to agreement on norms for scientific and engineering exchanges, or even to the development of a code of behavior. As already mentioned, the OECD could also provide important staff and analytical support for any new initiatives which the Western governments might take, in the common interest, to maintain closer watch over East-West economic relations.

This is by no means a full list of the international institutions which might play a supportive part in furthering East-West trade, nor have all the potentialities of those listed been fully developed. The leavening influence of these broader international bodies, whenever trade and financial relations between East and West are resumed on a sizable scale, should be able to contribute importantly toward the flow of these transactions. There are also, of course, literally a dozen bodies within the United Nations structure which have not been mentioned, but which might also have constructive roles to play in any revival of East-West economic relations.

The Potentials for Private Initiative
Most of the suggestions already made for governmental action, or for international institutions, would primarily serve to clear the way for the creative development of market opportunities by the business and financial enterprises of the West. Not all of these enterprises can properly be called "private," as there are a host of significant state-owned firms among the Western countries, particularly in Europe. "Private" here is a euphemism for firms operating in a market-guided — rather than a centrally planned — economy and which consequently have a wide freedom of choice among the resources they use, the products they produce, and the markets they serve.

The most uncomplicated exchanges are those involving the sale and financing of standard raw materials or fully finished products which trade at world market prices, and the short term finance related to their acquisition and transportation. While there is much room for expansion in such exchanges, by the '70s most of the procedural obstacles to the expansion of commodities trade were little different from the problems encountered among the market economies themselves (although the possible threat of policy-oriented interruptions of grains from the West or of energy or metals from the East did place these kinds of transactions under a slight cloud).

The particular difficulties which arise from the characteristic aspects of secrecy and planning rigidity in the CMEA countries could be accommodated by the same qualities of patience and persistence that are needed in building trade relations with many of the developing countries. It is chastening to realize, though, that in many East-West trading situations the better bargains have often been won by the

99

craftiness and skill of the traders from the East, assisted by the advantage in market power which monolithic state organizations have in dealing with fiercely competing private firms. This imbalance may indeed warrant somewhat greater collaboration among Western firms, possibly with government assistance (or at least forbearance) in order to cope effectively with the bargaining power of state-run enterprises.

The trading activities calling for more creative initiative, on both sides, appear when the products involved are more highly specialized, and involve the various aspects of advanced technology discussed earlier. In those circumstances, complex difficulties can arise, particularly in determining prices, but also in the specification of components, the organizing of material flows of components from several countries toward an assembly point, the transfer of machinery, or the setting up of whole plants with integrated production lines. There are also problems in agreeing on standards for inspecting and grading quality, in arranging credit terms (interest rates, payments dates, maturities, and the embedding of interest in the product prices), and in adjusting actual payments for delays or defects. To be sure, such problems arise in some form in many international dealings, but they are complicated by the layers of responsibility, and wariness about taking responsibility, within the bureaucracy of a monolithic state-owned economy.

In the early stages of any new business arrangements, particularly with the Soviet Union because of its vast size and often cumbersome procedures, delays are sometimes frustrating and the techniques gained from experience put a premium on keeping the same personnel continually assigned to the "Eastern connection." For that reason, smaller companies in the West simply cannot afford the "learning curve" of becoming active in trade with the East. For firms that can afford to persevere, there are still other opportunities in the form of turnkey plant construction, joint ventures, and licensing or leasing arrangements. For most of these, however, income is received through compensation agreements calling for repayments in kind rather than in cash. These can produce other kinds of headaches, for once an installation is in operation, repayment to the Western firm under such agreements may be made only by the delivery of goods produced in the new plant or with the new machine, or even by delivering other goods offered as payment in kind. Sometimes payments-in-kind may carry the added stipulation that such goods may be sold only in specified countries or markets abroad (where the Western firm may already have competing sales activity underway).

100

Nonetheless, despite the hazards, things do happen, and by the late '70s overall agreements for these more involved forms of cooperation had been made with the USSR by official bodies in some thirty countries in the West, in order to expedite and assist the efforts of their own national firms. Industrial cooperation agreements similar to those arranged with the USSR have also been widely established with the other CMEA countries. Actual joint enterprises, however, in which Western firms actually hold an equity interest and participate in management, have thus far been attempted only in Hungary, Romania, and to some extent in Poland. Bulgaria in 1980 prepared its legal procedures to provide a basis for such joint ventures.

Clearly, so far as Western enterprises are concerned, the spirit has been willing. The scope for fully realizing that potential, once the crises of 1982 abate, depends not only on the continued permissive or promotive support of the Western governments, but also on additional progress by the CMEA countries in developing more trade among themselves, more extensive trade abroad, and much more fluidity in the flow of convertible currencies within, and outside of, their own socialist community. The necessary condition for that spurring of growth which accompanies expanding trade is a flexible system of payments and credits among all of the participating countries. The CMEA countries are said to be eager and ready to widen the international division of labor in order to promote their economic growth; but they have not yet developed a payments mechanism, nor the facilities for a ready acceptance of direct investment from other countries on economic terms, that will permit such widening to occur on the scale that their underlying physical capabilities would permit. The combined initiatives of governments, international institutions, and private firms are necessary if these potentialities are to be realized.

CONCLUSION:
CONSTRAINTS AND OPPORTUNITIES

This study began by facing a challenging proposition: Since the East and West, even at the height of detente, remained adversaries; since the vigorous expansion of East-West trade during the '70s produced no significant change in the foreign policy of the Soviet Union; since both sides have continued enlarging their military complexes to increasingly menacing size—can there be any promising prospect for a renewed growth of economic relations between the Trilateral countries and the CMEA group in the '80s and beyond?

After nearly a year of working together, looking for both the pitfalls and potentialities of expanding economic relations with the East, the authors have reached three broad conclusions:

- Expanded trade would not weaken Western security. Expansion of trade within the limits of prudence would not add significantly to the military capabilities of the USSR or the Eastern European countries. Military requirements are largely met ahead of consumption. The trading policies of the Soviet and Eastern European regimes are now being forced to focus on providing more for the civilian sectors. Consequently, whatever might be added to the total incomes of the Eastern economies as a result of trade with the West is likely to flow to the civilian economy.

- Economic dynamism assures superior Western economic strength. Even though increased trade would assist economic growth in the East, as well as in the West, the Western economies will retain a wide margin of economic superiority, despite lapses into inflation and unemployment, as long as they maintain the flexibility and vigor of their market-oriented systems. The centrally planned economies, despite any useful gains from greater trade, seem unable to overcome the endemic problems of poor organization, waste, and inadequate incentives, which weaken their comparative economic performance.

- Expanded trade would provide valuable markets and resources for the West. The Trilateral countries can safely and profitably gain both new markets and new sources of goods by resuming an expansion of East-West trade when the current crisis subsides—

provided effective controls are maintained over the transfer of military technology, and provided there is prudent diversification of other sales and purchases.

These conclusions were reached against the background of anxieties created by the crisis in Poland. The resolution of the Polish situation, and the roles of both the Soviet Union and the West in that resolution, may well determine whether the CMEA countries move further toward economic interdependence with the West or whether there is a sharp turn toward the economic isolation and autarky of the 1950s.

If there is to be a renewal of trade, the binding limit is likely to be set by the ability of the East to export successfully into Western markets. Additional credits will not be available on the scale experienced during the past decade. Nonetheless, there is scope for mutually advantageous trade expansion along several lines, notably energy, agriculture, and technology. As the economies of both East and West recover from recent lethargy, trade can begin to increase with individual CMEA countries, and financial sources will again become available, based on the individual economic positions of each Eastern country and the particular projects to be financed. Financial support for trade could be reinforced by the IBEC and IIB, if their roles were to be enlarged by the CMEA countries as Eastern versions of the IMF and the World Bank.

With respect to energy, the Soviet Union has the reserves of oil, gas, and coal to provide adequately for most of the CMEA requirements and marginally for the needs of Western Europe and Japan. The related hard currency earnings by the USSR can provide a base for continued two-way trade with the West. There is not now, nor does there appear to be in prospect, an undue dependence by Western Europe on Soviet energy supplies. Careful monitoring and managing, however, will be needed to avert that danger.

On the other hand, the expansion of closer cooperation in energy may be a very positive development. The equipment needed in the East to produce and transport energy exceeds the presently foreseeable productive capacity of the Soviet Union and the countries of Eastern Europe. Sales of these goods to the East can provide a substantial market opportunity for the West. Moreover, as relations expand, both with respect to Western supplies of equipment and Eastern supplies of energy, the stake of each side in earnings from the other will increase. While neither side should, or is likely to, extend its commitments to a point of risking extreme vulnerability, a network of mutually beneficial exchanges in the energy field can encourage an added measure of restraint and orderliness in East-West affairs. What might, if overdone, become a trap of vulnerability for one side or the other can, if carefully managed, become a stabilizing linkage.

With respect to agriculture, gradually rising living standards throughout the CMEA countries have created an import requirement for grains and soybeans that is likely to be substantial for the indefinite future, although subject to considerable volatility from year to year. The Western governments, in encouraging their agricultural exports, should not provide subsidies for products shipped to the East and should avoid other policies that distort the natural operation of the markets. This, along with other active measures, should assist in stabilizing the volatile markets for agricultural commodities. There is also potential for the commercial transfer of Western agricultural machinery and methods to the East. In view of the immense and growing needs of the world as a whole for food, the export markets for the agricultural products of the West need not be impaired by the improvement of agricultural production in the East.

The import of technology by the East, to magnify the use and value of the human skills and natural resources which the CMEA countries have among themselves in abundance, can enable them to increase the output of their machinery, manufacturing, and mining sectors. That is vital if they are to earn, through exports, the funds to pay for their imports (including food) and to service their debt. From the Trilateral viewpoint, so long as there is no disclosure of critical military technologies, the sales opportunities in the CMEA markets are attractive. In turn, as CMEA exports grow, the Trilateral countries will have to be alert to market distortions created by CMEA dumping or by the monolithic bargaining power of state monopolies.

As for finance, while it clearly can serve an initiating role as trade is getting underway, credit from the West cannot be extended indefinitely. The Polish and Romanian situations in early 1982 underline the risks of over-extension and the danger of credit standards suffering from a competition in laxity. Yet the alternative of compensatory trade financing, useful as that can be for some individual projects, may already be approaching its limits. Indeed, when Western countries are required to take in payment the goods produced by equipment provided to the East on credit terms, the situation comes close to barter, with all the complications and inefficiencies that such a rudimentary economic system entails. Sizable and sustained expansion can occur only in conditions of relatively free trade, with products produced in the East finding their place in the world market by meeting the quality standards and fair trading practices of that market. When CMEA countries operate in that mode, they can also expect to benefit from a moderate increase in the level of outstanding credit from the West. Meanwhile, hesitancy in the West as to the availability of credit for the East will seriously limit the volume of trade.

Realistic prospects for the future require a balanced strategy, including policies or procedures that limit the scope for further trade, as well as those that support expansion. On the restraining side, an overriding priority for the West is to prevent or control the flow of critical military technology to the East. Present informal CoCom arrangements for the identification of critical products or technology are at times inadequate for borderline cases; the voluntary application of those criteria by individual countries is not always uniform. If at all possible, the fifteen countries participating in CoCom should formalize their arrangements through a specific agreement, ratified through treaties, and operated by a permanent, technically competent staff working under periodic review by senior government officials.

As another element of restraint, economic sanctions have had very limited effectiveness in the past. Sanctions are clearly inappropriate as a casual policy tool. They should be undertaken only in extreme cases, and then only if they can be sufficiently coordinated to have a meaningful effect. The countries associated with CoCom should be encouraged to develop a related set of procedures for coordination and consultation in the event that international developments justify consideration of sanctions. Such a group should attempt to define in advance a common Trilateral strategy outlining the procedures for implementing sanctions, and the conditions under which sanctions could be effective. The group should also provide for the sharing of burdens once sanctions are imposed—since the resulting costs of associated domestic sacrifices vary widely among countries and among sectors. If such arrangements are sufficiently firm to have genuine credibility, their mere existence may give the Trilateral countries enough negotiating strength to avert the actual use of sanctions in any given situation.

So far as policies to promote trade are concerned, both unilateral and multilateral efforts can be pursued. While government intervention can be useful in correcting market imperfections, and providing buffers against the stronger market power of state-owned agencies, governments must avoid intervening to provide concessional pricing either for products or for credits. There are potential roles, too, for such international institutions as the GATT, the IMF, the OECD, and the BIS.

Finally, from the Eastern side, a crucial contribution toward broadening the international division of labor throughout the East and the West could come through steps by the CMEA countries to extend the use of a meaningfully convertible ruble—initially among themselves and eventually with the rest of the world. The ultimate aim for the CMEA, subject to all of its own necessary political and strategic constraints, should be to move toward more open trade.

*　　*　　*

This study has wrestled throughout with the paradoxes of the Trilateral-CMEA relationship. It is sadly ironic that the two world communities with the greatest potentials in human and natural resources persistently obstruct the sharing of those potentials. Contrasting political systems and contending strategic aims restrain the natural tendencies toward a broader economic interdependence.

At the beginning of the 'seventies, economic forces seemed to be given new scope as the governments of the two sides took a series of steps toward political accommodation. The spirit of detente created in the West an illusion that political confrontation was being muted and that economic cooperation, as it flourished, would in itself provide a lessening of tensions. Such romantic notions have now subsided, and a new, constructive realism should take their place.

The world of the 'eighties initiates a new phase. Great power rivalry is at a crossroads. The turn can be backward toward aggressive confrontation, or it can be forward toward a measured interdependence. This study of the economic potentials for the years ahead finds promise in the prospects for a cautious, respected co-existence.

APPENDIX

Summary of Discussion
at Plenary of Trilateral Commission

TOKYO — APRIL 6, 1982

This task force report found many admirers and many critics when an earlier draft went before the meeting of the Trilateral Commission in Tokyo in April 1982. It is usual, particularly in a deeply controversial policy area like this one, that comments on a draft report concentrate on those elements or aspects of the report that commenting members find objectionable or inadequate — and the following summary will show that the Tokyo discussion of this draft report was no exception, particularly since we have omitted some of the more general statements of praise in order to concentrate on specific comments from the floor. Several interventions in the Tokyo debate were quite substantial and useful in illuminating the wider debate on these issues now underway, the purpose this summary is intended to serve. The authors found a number of the comments and suggestions extremely useful in making their final revisions; but after careful consideration, the main lines of argument in their Tokyo draft remain in the final text.

This summary (prepared by the Trilateral Commission staff) opens with comments on broad political or policy aspects of the issues involved, with much discussion of sanctions and how political strategy relates to economic relations. The sanctions after the Soviet invasion of Afghanistan and the new gas pipeline being built from the Soviet Union to Western Europe received considerable attention in these comments, in themselves and in relation to broader political or policy concerns. The summary closes with comments about problems businessmen and bankers face in dealing with the Soviet Union and Eastern Europe, and with comments about the functioning of grain markets during the Afghanistan sanctions and the large Soviet purchases since 1972/73.

Political Dimensions

This paper deals with an extraordinarily complicated and sensitive issue, one participant noted, on which there is a long history of disagreement and debate, not only between countries but within countries. There tends to be an almost natural division of opinion depending on one's own professional outlook or commitments; and this member recognized that his own professional and political experience condition what he has to say. There is an economic determinist framework that conditions the analysis of the paper, as this member sees it, and results in the underestimation of salient considerations. He focused on three areas where he felt more balance is needed.

The first pertains to the overall political context in which this issue needs to be considered. For the Soviet Union, the political dimension is critical, and we need to register more explicitly the fact that for a long time to come the East-West relationship, whether we like it or not, is going to remain competitive and occasionally intensely antagonistic. In a paper which is going to be read as a policy recommendation, it is odd, this participant argued, if we leave the impression that our overriding conclusion today is that we can expect and indeed propound a steady expansion of East-West trade in the foreseeable future. His own judgment of the likely character of the East-West relationship is more pessimistic: We are in a phase of intensifying antagonism, greater unpredictability, and probably occasionally sharpened conflict.

It is in this context that this participant found the discussion of the Afghanistan sanctions particularly simplistic and one-sided. The Western response to certain forms of Soviet behavior cannot be either a military response only or complete passivity, he argued, perhaps covered by a thin veneer of moral condemnation. Something in between is necessary, and the economic dimension offers that "in-between." It is simply wrong to condemn the policy of sanctions as a failure, unless one entertained the politically naïve idea that sanctions would drive the Soviets home. No one involved in shaping the policy of sanctions entertained such a simplistic notion. A more sophisticated version of that argument is also unacceptable — that the damage inflicted on the Soviet Union by sanctions must be greater than the benefits of the actions the Soviets undertook. It is very difficult to imagine the kind of economic sanctions that could drive the Soviets out of Afghanistan if the Soviets concluded that their strategic interests dictated that they be in Afghanistan. Does it follow therefore that our response should be of the military type? Or alternatively, that there should be no response if the economic response is incapable of inflicting sufficient damage on the Soviet Union? The fact of the matter is that economic sanctions do have the purpose of inflicting some costs and of driving home to the Soviet Union the seriousness with which a particular action is viewed, so as to diminish the likelihood of repetition. Some of the sanctions taken after the invasion of Afghanistan, particularly the grain embargo, did have significant costs for the Soviets involving discomfort and disruption. Obviously it would have been better if others followed, but that leads to the next point. It has been suggested that sanctions should be pursued only if there is close to unanimous consensus in favor of such sanctions, and unanimous participation in them. That is a prescription for doing nothing, because we know that there will never be such unanimity. The question then arises: Should the country which has some capacity for inflicting sanctions on its own, and has a major political interest in doing so, abstain because unanimity is lacking? What would have been the reaction of the Europeans to American policy on the Soviet aggression in Afghanistan, this member asked, if the United States had not imposed any sanctions at all on the grounds that the Europeans were not prepared to follow? The chorus condemning the United States for weakness would have been overpowering.

The second range of considerations which seems underemphasized in the draft, this member argued, pertains to the strategic implications of the problem. We have to face the fact that the Soviet Union has been spending a very high proportion of its GNP on a sustained military buildup, with strategic and political implications that cannot be ignored. In that effort, some aspects of technology transfer are important to the Soviet capacity to overcome bottlenecks and to advance their military capability. This point needs to be emphasized much more explicitly, especially since in recent months more systematic study of this issue has been generated. Another strategic aspect which is not given adequate consideration pertains to the problem of strategic vulnerability of the West resulting from certain connections, the gas pipeline in particular. We have to face the fact, this member argued, that any Western country dependent on the Soviet Union for 4 to 6 or 7 percent of its total energy supply is going to be affected by how the Soviets view the action it may be contemplating. No government would with indifference consider the possibility of suddenly losing so much of its energy supplies. This does give the Soviet Union leverage previously denied to it. It does create a new strategic relationship, in the context of a less favorable military relationship. Perhaps it is too late to consider any alternatives to the pipeline, but he still fails to see why some alternatives could not be devised in the context of an oil glut and of possible alternatives in Norway, Holland, Nigeria, Algeria and the United States. Maybe it is too late, but if it is too late, we should at least not deceive ourselves on the implications of what has taken place.

The final area in which this member felt some accommodation in emphasis needs to be undertaken is in the economic area itself. The Soviet economic system is in a state of growing crisis. It is a system which has run out of momentum. As it has entered the stage of economic complexity, it has found it more difficult to sustain its growth. It requires closer relationships with the West to a degree that previously was not the case, particularly in the area of advanced technology in order to overcome internal bottlenecks. These issues do have political significance, and in the context of growing tensions of a social-political type within the Soviet bloc, they are likely to become more important. Poland certainly is a classical example of massive systemic failure; and systemic failure which has political implications.

In sum, this participant concluded, it is the political dimension which is badly lacking in this draft, which gives it an unbalanced quality. The draft gives the impression that economics for the sake of economics is the point of departure for dealing with this sensitive issue in the East-West relationship, and this does not do justice to the manifold and complex character of that relationship.

Political Strategy in Use of Economics
Another participant also stressed the absence of what he considered to be the appropriate political context. He stressed that sanctions and restrictions on technology transfer, and some of the other things mentioned in the paper as means of guiding economic relations, do not constitute a strategy. They constitute occasional application of certain processes of denial, but they do not address the much more difficult and much more controversial issue (reflected, for instance, in the pipeline and the grain trade) of how we in the industrialized Western world might seek to shape the growth of economic relations with the Soviet Union in a way that is not only commercially tenable and advantageous, but also makes a contribution to the shaping of overall relations. With regard to the pipeline and other major programs of investment in the Soviet Union, we must ask ourselves whether this is the right strategy to pursue for the Western industrialized countries. The Soviet economy is declining in growth, in very large part because of the heavy investment in defense-related matters and the relatively heavy emphasis on consumption. What has happened for years is that capital investment has been squeezed; and this is very largely the source of the decline in Soviet growth that we have seen over the last several years and will continue to see. The question, as this participant sees it, is whether it is a wise Western strategy to help fill the investment gap that Soviet policy choices themselves produce, and to make it easier for the Soviet Union to overcome the decline in growth and decline in productivity with major capital investment ventures like the gas pipeline. That is a broad issue that cannot be determined by an individual firm or a group of firms, or an individual bank or groups of bankers. They are in the business of making business, not in the business of making national strategy. Such issues need to be discussed and resolved at a governmental level. This member's fundamental concern about the paper is that it overestimates the role of economics and underestimates the need for a political strategy in the use of economics.

Political strategy in the use of economics is very difficult for Western democratic, free enterprise systems to cope with. It suggests very strongly (and correctly) that economic relations with the Soviet Union are not like economic relations with other countries. They have to be seen in the context of an adversary relationship of long standing. Consequentiy, what this paper needs to address, or what any effort to deal with matters of East-West trade needs to address, has to go well beyond issues of sanctions (which are a negative part of economic policy), well beyond issues of denial, well beyond questions of technical-strategic trade controls as under CoCom. It has got to go to the issue of overall strategy. What is it that we seek to accomplish, and what is it that we don't want to accomplish, and what sort of conditionality should be attached to our economic relationships with the Soviet Union? This is an area in which all of us — Americans, Europeans, Japanese, Canadians — have been badly deficient over the last ten years. We do not have the institutions for it, and even if we had the institutions, we do not have the will and the political readiness to address the problem. Unless we do, we will get into constant debilitating debates about this or that economic deal, about whether pipelines are desirable or not, about whether sanctions are effective or efficient or not, about whether the grain trade should be equated with the pipeline, and so on and so forth. We need a strategy. We need a concept of what these economic relations are supposed to be doing for us.

This member added a final point: One of the important Soviet impulses in pursuing the policy of detente in the 1970s was the recognition that the Soviet economy does not have the means by itself to provide the capital and the technology for growth and increases in productivity. The significance of the 24th Party Congress eleven years ago, where Brezhnev spoke about this, was that the Soviet leadership acknowledged that it would need to come out into the world in order to obtain the benefits of the international economic system. That is something that will face the new leadership in the Soviet Union as well. So we can waste no time in trying to tell the new leadership, whoever they are, what would be the terms under which they can deal beneficially with the West.

Politically Stabilizing Impact of Trade
In following the transatlantic discussion of the new gas project with the Soviet Union, another participant observed, one could easily gain the impression of a booming surge in East-West trade. In actual fact, trade with the East can more accurately be described as being in a political and economic trough. West Germany's exports to the USSR, for example, have fallen by some 25 percent in real terms since 1975. At the same time, the German share of overall OECD exports to the Soviet Union (which have been swollen by inflation and grain exports) has fallen by no less than six percentage points to approximately 16 percent. The Federal Republic's trade with the smaller Eastern European countries is in even worse condition, owing to their cheerless financial state. In this situation, even the new gas project can serve little more than a consolidating function by replacing part of the diminishing Soviet oil revenues with earnings from natural gas, thus avoiding a complete drying out of the USSR's trade with the West.

The political fuss over East-West trade, this participant continued, makes sense only for one of the many schools of thought: those who would force the Soviet Union to its knees by means of a full trade embargo and, if need be, would be satisfied with Soviet hard-currency bankruptcy. Those holding this view, which this participant does not share, would reduce Poland to the role of a kind of explosive charge for Eastern bloc finances.

The majority of people in the Federal Republic of Germany view East-West trade — in a carefully measured dose — as serving a politically useful purpose. The fact that its volume continues to contract to the nadir of political relevance is a matter of great concern. Exports from the West to Poland have been cut by approximately one-half; political leverage for influencing the situation there — however slight — is

110

shrinking proportionately. Trade is thus losing a good part of its politically-stabilizing impact at the very point in time when economic problems in the East and the West are growing, and at the same time that the temptation is naturally becoming greater to take advantage of the difficulties encountered on the other side of the East-West border in order to engage in economic blackmail. A consolidation of East-West trade at a level conforming to the present overall economic situation would be desirable from a political point of view; a politically motivated *coup de grâce* would be the wrong policy. On the other hand, there are no objections to having the Soviet Union take note of the natural reactions of the banking community to international uncertainties for which it itself is responsible (such as Afghanistan and Poland), but no one should demand that Western governments simultaneously refuse to issue the guarantees normal for export credits, thus for their part exposing trade to additional political risks. In the midst of everything, we must not forget that the Soviet Union is a continental power and that it imports only 1.5 percent of its GNP from the West.

This participant noted in closing that the times are rather unfavorable for well-orchestrated exercises of Western solidarity in the field of equally distributing the burdens of economic sanctions. Each of us has his own concerns, whether they be wheat or the pipeline. Would it not be better for the cohesion of the Alliance to view the dimensions of this trade with greater sobriety, to accept its political significance at least for some of the partners in the Alliance, and in the relationship to the East to attempt first of all to make progress in solving the most important arms and arms control problems? Also, we should pay more attention to agreements already reached among us: signals that business will not be conducted as usual in the wake of martial law in Poland, as well as improved CoCom coordination.

Judging the Utility of Boycotts

Another member noted that, as one who participated in framing the U.S. and the allied boycotts against Iran and the Soviet Union, he has reflected a good deal about the utility of such tactics. He does not fully agree with the authors of the report, and presented his views as follows:

- The utility of boycotts cannot be judged solely by reference to whether they are "effective" in the sense of reversing the action that provoked them.
- Boycotts should be judged by whether they relieve the international tensions caused by an aggressive action of another state without leading one party or the other to initiate or widen the use of armed force.
- For this reason, especially when employed against a great power, boycotts must not be so effective that they become intolerable to the target, and induce the target itself to respond with armed force.
- The best example of a boycott that was too effective was the U.S.-British-Dutch embargo against oil shipments to Japan during the year before Pearl Harbor. The Japanese military machine was wholly dependent on this supply of American and Indonesian oil, and when this supply was cut off, Japan invaded Indonesia, or at least accelerated its invasion plan. Moreover, many Japanese and American historians now believe that the embargo convinced Japan we would not stay neutral if the invasion of Indonesia occurred, and that it influenced the Japanese decision to attack Pearl Harbor at the same time.
- Boycotts against a great power, therefore, have utility if they impose a cost which requires a painful adjustment, but not if they impose so intolerable a cost that the target goes to war. This is especially important when the target is a superpower such as the Soviet Union.
- Boycotts also permit the state imposing them to express its indignation and relieve its need to take reprisal by other more dangerous means, such as armed

111

force. Boycotts can be useful because they make a moral statement. They can satisfy the need to make a response, and they can bring home to the target the strong disapproval of those who impose them. For this reason, the fact that they impose costs on the boycotter — perhaps greater costs than those imposed on the target — is not a decisive argument against them, because a moral statement that requires a sacrifice to make it carries more weight than one that does not. The American colonial boycotts against all trade with Britain were far more painful to the colonists than they were to the British, but that made them even more effective as a moral statement. This spirit of sacrifice provided the cohesion that led to the Declaration of Independence, and created sufficient support for our grievances with Britain to make the Revolution itself a success.

- Apart from their economic effect, which this member believes was greater than do the authors, the post-Afghanistan boycotts of the Soviet Union may have had a similar moral effect on their target, in part because of the sacrifice they required. They may have heightened Soviet concern about the widening of these boycotts, and this may have limited the magnitude of the Afghanistan operation. It may also have helped to deter a similar invasion of Poland.
- If we apply this standard to judge the utility of recent boycotts — for example our long-standing boycott of Cuba, the Soviet bloc boycotts of Yugoslavia and Albania, and the more recent American and allied boycotts of Iran and the Soviet Union — they did relieve international tensions by means short of war. For this reason, I am reluctant to conclude that nothing good can be said for these boycotts, or for some limited form of economic reprisal for the continuing repression in Poland — such as agreed limits on new credits — on which all the allies can agree. At the same time, to bring about an economic Armageddon for the Soviet bloc — even assuming we could do so — would bring us all closer to disaster.

The Impact and Wisdom of the Afghanistan Sanctions
Another member noted that he found himself much closer to the general drift of the report than some of the criticisms laid out above. The draft report is a thoughtful and useful product in a very tricky area. This member shares the general professional bias of economists against economic sanctions — the arbitrage possibilities are just too great — but he did find some weaknesses in the draft report's criticism of the post-Afghanistan sanctions.

First, he noted, the draft report leaves the impression that the impact on Soviet grain supplies was really very small. It says the net denial was only 2.5 million tons. The estimate at the time was that the Soviets had a capacity to import 38 million tons of grain a year (and that they would have bought more if they could have gotten it into the country). The draft report shows that, during the crop year 1979/80, they actually got in 31 million tons. It follows, this member suggested, that a much better estimate of the net denial in the relevant time frame would be about 7 million tons, not 2.5. Moreover, although a lot of arbitrage did take place (and was expected), that too imposed costs on the Soviet Union. First, it imposed costs of delay. (It took some months before they could reorganize their trade, and those were crucial winter months in terms of feeding the new animals born in the spring.) Second, they had to pay much more for the grain they did secure. (They were paying a 20 percent premium for Argentine corn, for instance, which they substituted in considerable volume for U.S. corn.) Third, they had to accept some fodder of a type that was inferior to what they wanted in order to make up their supplies. In sum, as this member sees it, the impression is quite wrong that, even as a punitive move, the partial grain embargo had a negligible impact.

Second, on the broader issue of whether the Afghanistan sanctions were wise, the draft leaves the impression, although it falls short of saying so explicitly, that the imposition of this embargo was a mistake. Everyone who thinks that, this member continued, should play the "thought experiment" suggested above. Suppose the United States in January 1980 had confined itself to representations through diplomatic channels, and representations in the United Nations, over the invasion of Afghanistan. What would have been the reaction around the world, and in particular in Europe? This member's guess is that the silent criticism, and perhaps even the vocal criticism, would have been very much greater than in fact it was. This is a *very* important thought experiment to play.

Finally, the authors of the report sometimes analyze sanctions in terms of only two parties (the party imposing the sanctions and the party against whom the sanctions are imposed), but there are a lot of important bystanders in the world. What would have been the reaction in the Third World if the West, and the United States as the putative leader of the West, had confined itself to purely diplomatic reactions? In this member's estimation, one of the most important psychological impacts of the grains embargo was on various friendly nations in the Middle East. In assessing the impact of embargoes, one cannot neglect the reactions of third countries who are "engaged bystanders," particularly in this instance when a non-aligned Moslem country was invaded.

Spectrum of Western Approaches
Another participant described a spectrum of Western stances in economic relations with the Soviet Union and Eastern Europe, proceeding from the least to the most negative approaches: proscribing transfer of military technology, sanctions, attempts to shape Soviet behavior and development in general, and economic warfare.

On proscribing the transfer of military technology, this participant found no disagreement that we ought not to aid Soviet efforts to build up their military capabilities by providing them with advanced Western technology. Certainly one of the limited number of Western advantages in the military balance is our technological superiority. CoCom does reasonably well at enforcing the present rules. It is probably more important to stop the leakage in violation of the present rules than it is to try to expand the scope of the present rules; and tightening up of the present rules is very important, this member continued, because the Soviets have significantly narrowed the technological gap by importation of Western technology. That is not to say that they steal everything in their military technology from us — they have a very strong indigenous capability — but they are gaining by transfers of Western capabilities in violation of the present rules.

At the other end of the spectrum, this member came down against the idea of economic warfare, that is the attempt deliberately to cause a collapse of the Soviet system by economic actions. Soviet autarky is such that economic warfare will not work, and any such attempts by the West would tend to bring the Soviet people closer to their leaders. If we attempt economic warfare, the Soviet government will be able to say to the Soviet people, your economic problems are not because the Socialist Marxist-Leninist system doesn't work, but because there are attempts by capitalists outside deliberately to destabilize the system, to starve us, and so forth. Moreover, any such attempt would certainly aggravate the Soviet leadership's present paranoia.

This leaves the in-between area of sanctions and attempting to shape the Soviet economy and Soviet political behavior by economic action. On sanctions, this member tended to agree with what the critics of the draft report have said. Sanctions work not necessarily by forcing a reversal of strongly held strategic decisions — that won't happen — but by making the other side think a little more the next time. It may very well be that the Soviet decision to have the Poles suppress the Poles, rather than have the Soviets suppress the Poles directly, comes from their surprise about, and to some degree the effectiveness of, the Afghanistan sanctions. With respect to shaping Soviet development and political behavior, that will be very difficult to do, but this member is convinced that it has to be examined and perhaps tried by *governments*. Individual businessmen clearly cannot try to have that effect.

This member suggested that the following procedures be given consideration:

- Limit the time of sanctions, because they decay in effectiveness anyway, and because that allows you to reimpose them later on for some other misdemeanor, rather like penalties in a hockey game.
- Loans should be made only if insured by governments and only with the permission of governments, and with no concessionary terms.
- Finally, the USSR and individual Eastern European countries should be treated differently depending on how the individual Eastern European governments behave.

In closing, this member stressed that sanctions should be preceded, as others have said, by major consultations. And decisions on these matters really have to be managed much more strongly by governments than they have been — and more effectively and with more continuity than the American government in particular has shown.

Strengthen CoCom, Avoid Sanctions

The report's proposed further development of CoCom to ensure the denial to the Soviet Union, so far as possible, of weapons and sensitive technology supporting military capability seems to be warranted under the circumstances, another participant concluded. However, the analysis with respect to the use and effectiveness of economic sanctions would *not* appear to support the conclusion that a coordinated plan and organizational arrangements should be developed to agree in advance on the sorts of circumstances in which sanctions should be considered, their possible nature, appropriate burden-sharing and so on. The likelihood of agreement being reached in these areas would appear to be limited because of the diversity of economic and trading interests involved. The results, if applied, would seem unlikely to be cost effective or worthwhile in relation to the efforts involved. This member's conclusion is that, short of war or threatened wartime conditions, or of a U.N.-approved embargo, sanctions should be avoided in international trade, not least for commodities so basic as food and energy.

On the contrary, in this participant's estimation, outside the limits prescribed by CoCom, the mutuality of interest between buyer and seller, and the prudent availability of credit, should be left to determine trade levels between the Soviet bloc and market economies. As suggested in the report, this trade should be developed without competitive subsidization of exports, whether agricultural or industrial, via concessional credits or otherwise.

Agreement on Sanctions, Shaping Soviet Development

Many of the issues raised in the above interventions were discussed in other, briefer interventions in the Tokyo debate. There were voices from each of the three regions, for instance, arguing for a greater degree of agreement among Trilateral countries before sanctions are imposed.

An American member noted America's lack of success in making its view the Trilateral view of sanctions (and of economic relations with the Soviet Union more broadly). The report reflects in part, he felt, this failure to reach any kind of broad agreement on the effectiveness and design of sanctions; and thus the proposal made in the report that some sort of framework be negotiated is a step forward. Some argue that sanctions will never be imposed if you have to get agreement; but without agreement, sanctions may be doomed to failure.

A Japanese member agreed with an earlier speaker that a call for unanimity on sanctions is a prescription for doing nothing, but he stressed that we have to have some "minimum common concept," some "minimum of common planning" *vis-à-vis* the Soviet Union and the Soviet bloc through prior consultation.

A European member stressed that Europe cannot be called upon just to follow (or not follow) after the fact of U.S. action. There must be more intensive consultations in advance. He went on to argue that potent economic sanctions may work against our goal. Certainly the Soviet Union would have increased economic difficulties, but we may end up with *increased* international tensions, reduced chances for arms control, and a hardening of reciprocal relations.

Another European took a much harder line, arguing that we need to go beyond denial actions to an overall political strategy for economic relations, as advocated by an earlier speaker. Our real problem, he argued, is to exercise leverage on Soviet decisions about allocation of capital and investment. There are four main burdens on the Soviets: credit rescue of Eastern Europe, buildup of armaments, development of agriculture, and development of Siberia. Helping the Soviets in the credit rescue of Eastern Europe and supplying agricultural commodities allows them to devote more resources to armaments — and there is a surfeit of armaments on the Soviet side already. The Trilateral aim should be to influence Soviet decisions on allocation of GDP. If we have this point in focus, everything can be deduced from it with regard to a meaningful strategy — and we need a strategy, not just denial actions. It is another question whether or not the conditions for such a strategy are at our disposal, but we should not come out with a paper that overlooks these aspects.

Another American member noted that the political consequences of the recent grain embargo are still being felt in the United States. The recent farm legislation passed by Congress calls, in effect, for sanctions against the U.S. Treasury if another grain embargo is imposed. According to this member's rough calculations, under this legislation the Treasury would have had to pay $20 billion to American farmers during the Carter embargo. This will sharply limit any use of selective agricultural embargoes by the United States in the future. Given European objections to sanctions that do not touch this principal American export, this legislation may severely cripple any future efforts to achieve collective action on sanctions.

New Gas Pipeline Project

Several other participants touched upon the gas pipeline project in one way or another. An American found himself to be one of the few people on the Western side of the Atlantic who thinks the gas pipeline is a desirable thing on its merits, leaving aside the argument of not making a big fracas with the Europeans over it. It is desirable on its merits, he argued, because the major probable threat to the West (as distinguished from virtual threats) is not from the Soviet Union but from disruptions in the Persian Gulf. We cannot assess something like the pipeline solely in the context of East-West relationships. It has to be put into the global context. Disruptions of energy supplies are still a very important threat to the West, and therefore any policy of diversification is a desirable one, including if necessary — though admittedly it is second best — Soviet supplies. The corollary of diversification to Soviet supplies, however, is that the Europeans should pay more attention than it seems they have to fall-back arrangements to deter the Soviet Union from even thinking that it has a component of leverage over Western Europe.

A European member raised doubts about some European fall-back arrangements. We should ask ourselves what additional leverage the Soviet Union would gain if it joins forces with Algeria, and what if Nigerian gas passes through Algeria on its way to Europe? Then some countries might be 60 to 70 percent dependent on gas supplies from these sources. For structural reasons, this would be a rather dangerous situation, even if it doesn't look that way as a percentage of total energy consumption. On another front, if Norwegian gas workers on the North Sea go on strike for only four weeks, we will have depleted all the back-up stocks we are counting on. Thus there are dangerous loopholes in Europe's protection against excessive dependence.

An American member stressed that gross dependence figures are quite misleading. It is sectoral and geographic dependence that could be much more severe in its implications. A European member saw no geographic vulnerabilities, given the very extensive (80,000 + km) Western European integrated natural gas grid, with extensive flexibility and good surge capacity. Some possible sectoral vulnerabilities do need to be examined, however, since gas is not easily or completely substitutable in some cases. To aid in crisis management mechanisms, this member hoped the authors would recommend that the United Kingdom allow gas exports and connect to the European grid. The authors might also want to recommend that the International Energy Agency, now studying natural gas imports, monitor our fall-back mechanisms. (The European Community could perhaps do some of this also.) This member agreed with the point made earlier that, in a comparison of risks, Soviet gas looks better than Persian Gulf oil. Also, the costs of reducing vulnerability look more favorable in the case of gas.

Primacy of Politics
A number of speakers stated their agreement with the point that the draft report was prepared too much from an economics or business point of view, and that politics should be given primacy in devising approaches to economic relations with the Soviet Union.

The draft report reminded one American member of the old line that "Christmas is over, and the business of business is business." He thought the American people would be impatient with the "business as usual" tone of the paper while they are being asked to make real sacrifices for rearmament. In a similar vein, the paper does not deal adequately with the problems that can result from the feeling in the United States that Europe puts more emphasis on its economic interests in dealing with the Soviet Union than on the Alliance's strategic interests — a feeling which lies behind Mansfield-type resolutions in Congress.

A Japanese member speculated on how the Chinese would react to the draft report: They would interpret it as a classic textbook case of the capitalist system, which just wants to pursue profit. The strengthening of this impression in China is not favorable for the strategy of our regions. Another political dimension that needs more attention would be the differences between Eastern Europe and the Soviet Union.

The draft report gives the Soviets the impression, one European member stated, that we shall soon be back to "business as usual." Another European was worried about the emphasis in the last major section on so many positive avenues for facilitating trade.

Another European stressed that there is no possible economic strategy of struggle with the Soviet Union if not contained within a global political and military strategy. As history shows (e.g., sanctions against Italy in 1935), economic sanctions by themselves are useless.

A Japanese member agreed that the draft put too much emphasis on economics, but he argued that we would not necessarily make our position more powerful by taking political aspects more into account. West Germany has to worry about Berlin and East Germany. Japan has to worry about the Northern Territories. Japan and

116

West Germany might feel themselves more inferior to the Soviet Union if these political concerns more fully informed their approach to economic relations. In the economic realm, the Trilateral regions are much stronger than the Soviet bloc. People worry about our economic dependence on them, but their economic dependence on us is much greater.

A European member stressed that economic and business considerations are only part of a much larger picture; and that we must make clear the overriding political, moral and other considerations determining our relationship with "the other side." He went on to note, however, that many European firms, such as in the steel sector, have to choose between complicated, not too advantageous deals with the East and closing down plants. They do business with the Russians not because they love them, but because of overriding business considerations.

One of the Europeans who argued the need to assert the priority of politics, went on to state — as did another member — that there should be more in the paper on the "North-South axis" in connection with East-West economic relations — in oil and energy, in finance and capital, and in other areas.

Business Costs and Risks in Soviet Trade

While the paper has a number of excellent suggestions for Trilateral governments in furthering economic exchanges, an American member stated, it needs a stronger emphasis on the role of private initiatives and the difficulties and risks they face. Ultimately trade will depend on corporations from the Trilateral countries signing contracts in which they can make a profit. The paper will be read by Ministry of Foreign Trade officials in Moscow, this member continued, and they should understand that trade is not just a matter of signing cooperation agreements and having understandings with governments. It requires creating an atmosphere in which those actually engaging in trade can find a way to make a profit. The paper will also be read by Trilateral businessmen; and they should realize how hard it is to do business with the Soviet Union in particular. The paper needs to emphasize the costs and risks more explicitly:

Costs: Maintaining an office in Moscow; extensive travel from Vienna and other cities from which trade is handled; repeated visits to continually re-negotiate contract terms; skilled efforts by Ministry of Foreign Trade officials to encourage protracted competition and discounting by the vendor companies in Trilateral countries; protracted delivery and installation schedules for technical projects. These costs make trading, particularly with the Soviet Union, more expensive than trading with most other countries.

Risks: For a private company in any one of the Trilateral countries, there are considerable risks in CoCom and more particularly U.S. export licensing procedures which may not become clear until after contracts are negotiated.

There are considerable risks in transferring technology along with products, not from future competition in Trilateral markets, but from copying of the technology and products, particularly in the Soviet Union, thus limiting the opportunity for follow-on sales. There are risks for private companies in spending time and money to negotiate contracts, only to find that competition from other Trilateral governments offering credit at lower interest rates causes the sale to be lost.

The paper overlooks one important problem faced by corporations in building relationships with the Soviet Union, although the same conditions do not exist as extensively in doing business with other Soviet bloc countries, or for that matter with the People's Republic of China. In the Soviet Union, it is extremely difficult to build relationships with end-users that can lead to profitable long-term relationships. The Ministry of Foreign Trade is very effective at isolating users in the Soviet Union from suppliers in Trilateral countries.

In sum, this member concluded, the costs are high, risks considerable, and long-term benefits questionable. No corporation in a Trilateral country should enter into business relationships with a Soviet bloc country without recognizing the substantial difficulties in the way of achieving acceptable profit margins. In fact, an objective in trade with the Soviet Union might well be to look for profitable targets of opportunity rather than for building long-term relationships. The paper might do well, in the private sector comments at least, to emphasize the fact that there are more obstacles in the way of trade with the Soviet Union than with other Soviet bloc countries.

Issues for Banks

A European member noted that differences among governments in attitudes toward lending to CMEA countries — between the softer line of West Germany, France and Italy and the harder line of the United States and, to some extent, the United Kingdom and Australia — are creating difficulties among banks. We may see divergences among banks wanting to reflect policies of their home governments, and these divergences among banks could cause trouble in rescheduling and in new credits for Eastern Europe. This member stressed the different position banks are in with CMEA borrowers relative to other Euromarket borrowers — the IMF cannot step in as a lender of last resort (except perhaps in the case of Romania). Even if the CMEA countries were all IMF members, it is not clear they would be able to follow IMF dictates with regard to their economic policies. The "umbrella theory" might apply in reverse — one CMEA country's difficulties may affect the standing of all of them. The rapid expansion of the 1970s is likely to be replaced with a cautious and wary approach in the 1980s, with banks concentrating on reducing their exposure.

Another European member emphasized the difference between credits to the Soviet Union and credits to national companies doing business with the Soviet Union. His bank recently refused to join in a credit to the Soviets for the new pipeline, but it does provide credit to West German companies for this project, if the loans are backed by West German government guarantees. This underlines that the real decisions come from political authorities.

Agriculture

Two American members concentrated on the agriculture section of the report in their comments. We should not overestimate, one of them stressed, the effect of the partial grain embargo on the drop in U.S. farm net income between 1979 and 1980. If Soviet grain imports were only 2.5 million tons less than they would have been in the absence of the embargo — world grain trade in 1979/80 was 196 million tons and U.S. exports were 94 million tons — it is hard to believe that such large price and income effects could have resulted from so small a relative aberration. And the grain markets seem to have agreed with the view that the embargo had little effect upon world and U.S. exports of grains. The price of U.S. wheat in Rotterdam in December 1979 was $ 212 per ton; the lowest price for the year was $188 in April 1980 and by July the price was back to the December 1979 level. Corn prices were affected even less, declining from $139 in December 1979 to a low of $129 in January 1980 and recovering to the December level by May and June 1980. It is true that U.S. grain stocks increased during 1979/80 — from 72 million tons to 75 million tons. This increase represented a little less than 2 percent of U.S. domestic use plus exports.

The discussion of the 1972/73 grain imports by the USSR, this member continued, gives a seriously distorted picture of the events of 1972/73 and the next two or three years. There is no mention of the U.S. export subsidy on wheat which significantly

118

interfered with the functioning of the market. If there had been no export subsidy, the price developments would likely have been very different. Since 1972/73 there have been four years in which the USSR has imported more grain than during 1972/73 and there have been no price developments similar to those of 1972 and 1973. It might be appropriate for the authors to explore why world grain markets have been able to absorb rather easily the large and erratic Soviet grain imports in recent years.

The second American member also stressed that the draft report exaggerates the contribution of Soviet purchases to price instability and market disruptions. Soviet purchases in 1972/73 constituted only about one-half of the increase in export demand for that year, and this increase in export demand accounted for only about one-half of the price increase that year. Whatever one thinks of the impact of those purchases then, a number of developments since have reduced the likelihood of disruption: The end of the U.S. export subsidy has led to smaller individual sales and meant that sellers cover their sales more quickly (with, therefore, more rapid market effects); physical limits on Soviet imports reduce possible fluctuations; and the market has become more experienced and sophisticated, even though the Soviets have not come through with much information on production, consumption and stocks.